Weezie

A Palm Beach Story

Fraud, Lies & a Colombian Mystery

Louise Ford

ISBN-13: 978-1456540746

ISBN-10: 1456540742

For my darling Nellie,

— All my Love,

Weezie

This book is dedicated with love to:

Peter McDermott

Nick & Alanna Grant

Acknowledgements

I also want to thank:

Mary Dearborn for her editing and help in so many ways.

My legal "team" Sam Troy, Joel Hirschhorn & Jhan Lennon (as a
very supportive legal friend!)

With sincere apologies to anyone I may have missed, special
thanks to (in alphabetical order):

George & Vee Angle, Junie Augsbury, John Bocciolatt, Nellie
Benoit, Patricia Clarke (much missed), Jackie Cowell, Anne
Rodney D'Janeoff, Barret & Trey Gargano, Pamela Goldsack,
Debby Gregg, Brigadier James Ellery, Rexford & Janet Ennis,
Susan Ferguson, Katy Keiffer, S. Halcro Kinder, Polly Lyman,
Margaret Lumley-Savile-Patre, Lauren & Renato Sarti, Juliana
Seeligson, Ruth Anne & Charlie Shields, Shirley & David Taylor,
Paula Watters and Tory Watters.

For giving me the courage and encouragement to write my story.
Every word of which is true!

Table of Contents

Prologue
Weezie: A Palm Beach Story
and
The Colombian Mystery

In August 2010, as I was finishing up the work on this book, my wonderful editor Mary V. Dearborn and I had a conversation where I suggested that we should give Bea Ford the opportunity to clear up any of these very glaring discrepancies in legal documents that I had uncovered while researching for this book.

Mary called Bea in her Newport RI summer home, telling her who she was and that I had written a book and would like to know if she would like to comment on a few things that I had uncovered. Her first question was "Why do you have two different birthdays on legal documents?" Mary said there was dead silence and Bea replied "That is private and I don't discuss private matters on the telephone. Weezie has my address." She then hung up without saying goodbye!

That was fine, so Mary happily wrote to Bea asking the same questions she was going to ask on the phone. There was no response.

§

At the end of October, over two months later, when I had finally gotten most of the last bits of this book finished I sent Bea a manuscript to let her see it and give her one last opportunity to comment, correct, deny etc., anything she might want to. The manuscript arrived at her house in Palm Beach and was signed for on November 3rd 2010.

§

On November 1st without knowing the manuscript was already on its way Faxon Henderson who has been Bea's legal advisor though all of the changes to my fathers documents sent a letter via snail mail to Mary which she received, scanned and sent to me on November 8th. In it he stated that "Bea reserves her rights to privacy and privilege and has no wish to make any comment on my book".

I replied, again by snail mail, as I guess this is all Mr. Henderson has, that was fine and I would now proceed to publish.

§

On December 8th 2010, my editor Mary Dearborn, received a phone call from Thomas Julin, Esq. Mr. Julin said he represented my father's widow, Beatriz. Mr Julin asked Mary various questions about the book and whether Mrs. Ford could "work with me on this". Mary told Mr. Julin he would have to talk to me directly and she got an email address from him. I then sent Mr. Julin an email on Dec 8, 2010 and he replied immediately to thank me for making contact with him.

§

Then on December 16, 2010, I received a call from Mr. Julin at my house in England. I wrote immediately to Jhan Lennon, Esq. an attorney in Boca Raton, Florida and a family friend. I let Mr. Lennon know that Mr. Julin had called and asked me if I might want to make a deal about my book. Mr. Julin had also asked me what it would take to not publish my book.

Mr. Julin informed me during this phone call that he was meeting with Beatriz the next day and he would like me to put together something to present to his client. I told Mr. Julin, on the phone, that I was very surprised that he had called me at this late date since it had been many months since I first tried to discuss the content of my book with Bea. So at that point it was probably too late to change anything as I had done extensive research and was happy with my content and its accuracy.

After some prodding from Mr. Julin and while I hemmed and hawed, saying I had not given it much thought, it would be nice to have both of my father's houses put into trust and willed back to me by Beatriz when she dies. Mr. Julin replied "That's it? You just want something when she dies? " I then said, "Well I guess I might be making some money off this book so some compensation now might be nice but I have no idea what it should be and that I had to talk to my partner and get back to him."

It was after that conversation that I decided to retain an attorney and Jhan Lennon kindly provided me the contact information of Samuel R. Troy, Esq. Mr. Troy then contacted Mr. Julin and also discussed this matter in full with famous attorney Joel Hirschhorn, Esq. in Miami.

There was too-ing and fro-ing on this between Mr. Julin, Mr. Troy and Mr. Hirschhorn.

Finally Mr. Julin sent this email, attached below, to my attorneys. It states that Mrs. Ford and her Family do not consent to Louise Ford publishing FACTS about them! For me this simply confirmed that everything I have written in my life story is absolutely true.

As Joel Hirschhorn said to me yesterday. January 6th 2011, in his office "The great thing about America is the First Amendment!"

Sam -
Beatriz Ford does not consent to publication by Louise Ford of any facts about her or her family members. She also declines to respond on a point-by-point basis to Louise's threatened publication of her book or to pay Louise not to publish the book. She reserves all of her rights.

Thomas Julin
Partner
Hunton & Williams LLP

Chapter 1

Beginnings:
Rochester and Lake Placid

I may have been precocious, but I was never spoiled. I cannot say I was given whatever I wanted, showered with love and affection, or made to feel like a princess, as all little girls—and for that matter, big girls—dream.

Oh, on the outside, I had all the trappings of the spoiled little rich girl, but the reality was that I was a very lonely child with two parents who were caught up in their social and sporting lives, even after I made an appearance. Though it was the era of the nanny—and I did have Ursula, a German baby nurse, until I was four—my parents always took me along for the ride. Whether that ride was on skis, on board the Venture, or in shooting parties, I went along.

I was raised by my mother's steady diet of conversations over iced vodkas, Manhattans, and grasshoppers.

Grasshoppers were the favorite drink of my ninety-something- year-old Aunt Sadie, my maternal grandmother's sister—a Gavin. She was the only one left of the generation of my grandparents, both of whom died before I was born. My mother's mother had married my grandfather, Williams F. Watters, who was a judge at the turn of the century. He was successful in many business ventures, but what he loved best had to do with the new motorcars. He owned a few automobile dealerships over the years and was the first commissioner for motor vehicles in NY State. I may never have known my grandfather, but my son Nick and I inherited his love of cars and boats—anything that moved with a motor.

My grandparents treated their first child Mort, as if the sun rose and set on his wishes. Born in 1910, Uncle Mort graduated from Georgetown University, where he met and married Bernice Baylis, the daughter of a brigadier general. He grew up to be a pioneer in broadcasting. My Uncle Mort had two daughters with Bernice, Mary Ellen and Rosemary. When I was eight he and Bernice divorced and he married Paula Jane. Together they had one daughter Victoria (Tory).

My mother, Mary Louise, was born in 1917. She had a happy childhood in the shadow of her older brother, but he went away to boarding school when she was seven. She was second generation at Sacred Heart in Rochester and a great athlete. She had many friends who she kept her entire life. When she was just fourteen, she drove her mother, Rose, all the way from Rochester to California for the winter, a trip that must have taken weeks. Moreover, at a time when cars seldom ran more than fifty miles without needing mechanical attention, my fourteen year old mother fixed the car on the way.

My father, George E. Ford, was born in 1907 in Barrie, Ontario, an only child. At twelve, his lots his mother and father to the flu epidemic of 1917-1919, and he was given the choice of living with his grandparents in Toronto, or with an aunt in Rochester, NY. His grandparents were strict, and he remembered his aunt as having given him many presents, so like any bright twelve-year-old, he chose the aunt. After the move to Rochester, however, he found out that his uncle was a drunk, and he struck out on his own by the age of sixteen, working his way through the University of Rochester School of Engineering.

Dad's earliest love was sailing, and in the 1930s, he led the US team that raced 14' dinghies all over Europe. He brought the International 14' class back to the USA, having purchased the RIP from Stewart Morris at Cowes.

My father worked for Rochester Manufacturing Company/Taylor Instruments until 1940, when he married my mother, Mary Louise Watters. She must have seemed the perfect partner. Dad was a great outdoorsman, having learned to sail with his grandfather at the Royal Canadian Yacht Club at a very young age. He was most at home walking in the woods, ruffed grouse hunting with his dogs, skiing, and horseback riding then in any city.

My mother was a great sportswoman and had been a college tennis star at Manhattanville. She was a champion skeet shot and a great skier. Her family had a summerhouse on Lake Ontario, where she learned to sail or operate any boat under power better than most men.

Sometimes I wished I had a mother like everyone else's, in a bright and flowery Lilly dresses and Pappagallo shoes. My mother owned plenty of those, but her looks were more classic, straight out of Ralph Lauren—only decades earlier. Like young Katherine Hepburn, she wore grey flannel trousers with a Brooks Brothers shirt, blazer and a pair of Bass Weeguns. She only cared to look classic and was not obsessed with fashion. On her wrist, she wore a gold Omega watch, and the only other jewelry she wore her one good string of pearls and simple pearl earrings, along with a large emerald-cut diamond and her diamond wedding band. Her only other ring, worn on her right pinky, was a two-carat diamond in a gold setting. This diamond had been one of a pair that her grandmother had worn as earrings; her cousin Rosemary had the other. I was heartbroken, when at twenty-two, apparently while taking off a pair of gloves in a London taxi, I lost this ring, of many sentimental things I would lose.

§

My parents married in 1940, but they would not have me for fourteen years, when my father was forty-eight and my mother thirty-eight. I was born at the end of 1954. My mother suffered repeated miscarriages trying to conceive me. The doctors finally gave her DES the wonder drug of the 1950s. DES enabled her to carry me full-term but it started a sequence of events that would continue to kick me in the ass for the rest of my life.

I was a cherished and overprotected child. After their marriage, my parents lived in a brick house they built themselves on a lovely piece of property with an apple orchard on what was originally a dead-end street. When I was two, they learned that the street was to be opened up, and they began looking for a new house rather than have me hit by a car on a through street. They went house-hunting and found another house on a dead-end street, Indian Spring Lane, in Rochester, New York, a house my parents always told me they chose not only for its safe location, but because there was a little girl my exact age, Connie, who lived next door. The house backed up to the seventh tee of the Country Club of Rochester golf course. It was a great spot to grow up in. The entire golf course became a year-round playground, providing big woods, a great creek to catch polliwogs in, and miles of open space on which to ramble. There were also other kids my age on the street. Randie Jackson was two years younger than Connie and I lived on the bend in road. Randie was the youngest of five girls and Connie the youngest of four. Chippy Weismiller was always experimenting with something that might blow up in his garage. It was something kids did then and no one took any notice. Paula, Harry, and Andrew Sullivan lived across the circle from me. Harry was a year older than Connie and I. His mother was the very glamorous, beautiful blond Jackie Sullivan who had studied at the Sorbonne. She drove a chocolate-colored Cadillac convertible. I thought she was the bee's knees. She now lives in Palm Beach with her second husband Dick Cowell and is still incredibly beautiful and a great friend to me.

My parents seemed ancient when I was growing up. It seemed like everyone else had mothers that were so much younger. Mine had grey hair, and most of my parents' friends had grandchildren my age. I longed to be like my best friend Connie, who lived next door and was the youngest of four girls. She had her big family around for dinner every night.

When my parents first married in 1940, my Uncle Mort and my grandmother Rose loaned my father seed money to start his own company, Qualitrol Corporation, which made gauges and control devices for electrical transformers. By the time we moved to the Indian Spring house, my father rarely had to travel on business any more, having delegated most of the company's operations to others. He hired Harry Rice, who had a daughter my age named Callie, to be VP of Qualitrol. Dad thought the world of him.

§

After I turned twelve and left Sacred Heart, my mother felt she had to stay home with me, and our golden days as a sporting family were seemingly over. My father began to travel more and more often on sporting trips, leaving my mother home alone with me. Rosemary, my Aunt Sadie's daughter and my mother's double cousin (because two Watters brothers married two Gavin girls), were very close. During this time, my mother and I spent a lot of time with Rosemary; her husband, Art Lohman; and Aunt Sadie, who lived with them.

My mother hated to cook. The only thing I remember her cooking Marie Eisle, would sometimes leave dinner for us when she went home for the day, but we went to one of my parents' clubs for dinner at least three or four times a week. This pattern continued even after my mother died when I was fifteen. Dad would take off, leaving me for extended periods with Marie and her husband Frank, who were German immigrants. Marie had come to the US at the age of twelve after WWI and went to work as a live-in servant on the same street on which my mother grew up. She was the same age as my father, born in 1907, so she was ten years older than my mother was. Neither remembered the other from Dartmouth Street.

I don't know if any other family members came over with Marie, or if she was brought over to be a servant. She never talked about her family, other than her children, and she hated Germany and never wanted to go back. Frank worked in a factory called Schlagel, where I think many other German immigrants worked.

Marie was a class act—hard working, gracious, kind and a loving woman who in some ways was more a mother to me than my own. She washed my hair until I was fourteen. She used to make macaroni for dinner, and Frank would put ketchup on it (which grossed me out). She also made homemade egg custard, baking it in a pan of water in the oven; it would get almost a crisp crust on the top, which was sprinkled with nutmeg. I wish I knew how to recreate it.

Marie started working for my mother before I was born and stayed on until my father and Bea sold the house in Rochester around 1975. Both she and Cliff—Cliff, who would later work for us on Grindstone Island—left because they could not stand working for Bea, who treated everyone who worked for her very badly. They had both adored my mother and could not understand how my father could have married a woman so unlike my mother.

Marie was terrorized by the teenager left in her care. We used to smoke pot in front of her, telling her it was Indian cigarettes. I once had a party, to which hundreds of kids from all over the place came. It was right out of a high school movie. If Facebook had been invented, it would have been one of those parties that people announce on their Facebook pages. During the party, I walked from room to room without knowing a single face. We left the house a total mess, and at six AM, Marie was awake on her hands and knees, scrubbing her kitchen floor. I have never gotten over doing that to her. It brings tears to my eyes just thinking about it.

I have great memories of how much Marie and I loved each other. When the Beatles' "I Want to Hold Your Hand" came out, my mother, overprotective as always, wouldn't let me get it. On the other hand, Marie, a huge Elvis Presley fan, understood how important it was for me to have it and bought it for me, the first 45 record I owned. I had a big playroom in the basement of the house on Indian Spring Lane, where my record player was kept. I have no idea if my mother ever knew that Marie had gone behind her back to get me the record. Nothing was ever said.

Connie and I, and sometimes Randie Jackson from across the street, spent hours and hours down in the basement. I had a big rocking horse, and Connie and I often played Roy Rogers and Dale Evans. She was always Roy. We also roller-skated down there and put on plays that we made Marie and my mother suffer through.

Dad built me a big playhouse in the wooded area between our lawn and the seventh tee of the CCR golf course. Connie had a playhouse, too, but it was smaller than the big one Dad made me, so we hung out at mine. She and I would make mud pies and try to talk Randie, two years younger than us, into eating them. I have a wonderful photo of Connie and me, age four-ish, sitting on the lawn, arms around each other, in front of a pile of grass and dandelions we made into the shape of a big nest. In it, we put two white eggs from the fridge and called our mothers out to see, announcing that we had made this nest, and birds had come and laid eggs in it.

To the extent that they still felt they could, my parents continued to take me wherever and whenever they went to have fun. Every winter until I was twelve, they took me out of my school, Sacred Heart, for two months to join them at the Lake Placid Club in the Adirondacks. (Looking back, I don't think this made me very popular at school. I doubt it helped that my overprotective mother picked me up at school every day in her big Cadillac, while all the rest of my friends, including Connie, rode on the bus, talking and laughing.)

My parents had an enormous social circle and picked up their usual pace as soon as we got to the Adirondacks. I continued to be dragged into the middle of it, but increasingly, I chose to wander around the giant old Lake Placid Club by myself, much like Eloise at the Plaza—except that Weezie at the LPC didn't have a turtle.

I made fantastic friends with our maid Blanche, who used to bring hot, milky coffee to work with her in a thermos. She and the other maid on the floor would sit in the linen closet, the room where our Christmas ornaments were stored in boxes on the top shelves. They had a small wooden table in it, two chairs, and a rocking chair. They took their breaks in this glorified broom closet, letting me have the rocking chair. The smell of that coffee is still strong in my nostrils today. I would rock happily, listening to them talk about their families and how cold it was walking to work each morning. I remember Blanche saying that her eyelashes froze in the -30F temps outside. I loved sitting and listening to those women. They always brought me extra coffee cake.

Some of my fondest memories of the club are of riding in the elevator with the elevator men. At the insistence of my father, who worried about fire, we lived in a club building called Agora, the only part of the club that was built out of brick, newer than the main old wooden club house. (My father was proved right when the rest of the Lake Placid Club, having sat abandoned for years, burned to the ground in the1980s.) The elevators were those wonderful old-fashioned ones, which you only see in places like Paris now. They had cage doors that crashed shut and handles on semicircular disks. The operator would push the handle forward (or counterclockwise) to go up and backward (or clockwise) to go down. The elevator men could make the elevator go slower or faster, and sometimes they let me push the handle. One of the two elevator operators had a daughter who was close to me in age, and I spent some time playing with her. (I doubt the club approved of the employee's kid hanging around much, but I was thrilled to have company at the time.)

I was also great friends with a girl named Mary Claire Carroll, whose father was the club secretary. She was a couple of years older than I was, but I loved hanging out with her. The first thing I would do when my family arrived in the winter was call her on the club phone and see if she could come over. Her older sister Kathleen was a film critic in NYC, very glamorous to us, and an older brother went to Viet Nam.

My parents and I always had the same table and waitress in the dining room for all the years we stayed there. The table was right by the enormous windows that looked out over the swimming pool and tennis courts. The tennis courts were flooded in the winter into a giant ice skating rink. The club had these old ice push chairs from the Victorian era. We had fun skating as fast as we could, pushing each other and dumping the rider into the snow banks or spinning them around and around.

Just outside the window below our table in the dining room was a man I seem to remember as an Indian, who came every day with his dog sled to give rides to anyone staying at the club. Because they had two eighteen-hole golf courses and lots more land, this was a wonderful thing to do. Year after year, we sat at the same table; our waitress's name was Mabel; like so many of the staff, Mabel was my friend. When I was a little girl, my nurse Ursula and I were allowed to eat ahead of everyone else, so I used to watch the waitresses all line up and be inspected by the maître d' before the doors opened to everyone else.

One of my favorite things about eating a meal in that dining room was the women who wore metal contraptions on their chests that looked a lot like accordions. They were actually heated ovens with a roll-up door on the front—like a roll top desk—and inside was an assortment of hot rolls, Melba toast, and my favorite, sticky buns. I miss these women and the other workers even now. My heart is full of wonderful memories of life at the LPC. I don't think any other club was quite like it then and certainly not now. The people at the club made a great impression on a little girl, and made her life there a lot less lonely.

Aside from the being at the LPC with the "Febs" for the month of February, we also spent every Christmas there until I was eighteen, the club was no longer a club, Mom was gone, and it was just over. Until then, Christmas at the Lake Placid Club was magical. We had a big tree in our room and all our old ornaments were there waiting for us year after year. Three or four days before Christmas, the club would hold a Yule log hunt. We would all bundle up in our warmest snowsuits, with multi-colored capes with hoods on them, and trudge off into the woods singing Christmas carols and hunting for this log. I don't think we actually hunted the log at all, and I remember the log not having any bark on it. It had a huge notch carved into two sides of it so a rope could be tied around it and we could all drag it back. It seemed very large.

§

On Christmas Eve, there was a big pageant and ceremony in the Agora theatre. The Yule log was brought in and placed in the huge fireplace to the left of the large room. When I was older, I as one of the three or four kids who read a Christmas tale, I think German stories, and hold pine boughs that when we were done reading we threw them into the fire over the burning Yule log so they would pop and crackle. There was also a wassail ceremony, which involved everyone getting out of his or her seats, and going and getting a cup of wassail while everyone sang "Here We Go a-Wassailing." I loved drinking the wassail. I don't know if it had alcohol in it because they served it to everyone, but in those days, it might have.

Last, but not least, there was a Christmas pageant on the stage. There was a wooden stable with a manger, the baby would be put in it, and an assortment of kids played the different parts. I was, depending on my age, an angel or a shepherd. I never made it up to be Mary. By then, I was one of the Yule log readers. Then it was off to bed for us little ones. When we woke up in the AM, the tree in my parents' room was loaded with presents under it. One year, my parents' room had been painted. My father was allergic to paint and took a smaller room down the hall. On Christmas Eve, while looking through the key hole in the door, I saw my father coming down the hall with all the presents. That was how I found out about Santa Claus. No matter, because for many years, the highlight of Christmas morning was Santa coming after breakfast to Agora and handing out presents to all the kids there.

§

On New Year's Eve, there was another big pageant. Up until midnight, all the chairs were taken out of the Agora theatre, an orchestra played, and everyone danced and danced. A few minutes before midnight, the merriment stopped, and Old Father Time walked across the stage. Dressed in white robes and white beard with a sickle over his shoulder, he trudged across the stage, and the clock counted down the seconds until midnight. Right at midnight, there was a big kaboom; balloons rained down, and up high on a balcony over the fireplace, where the Yule log had burned, appeared the New Year's Baby. There was always some small baby in the crowd of over a thousand who stayed in the club and its many "cottages" for New Years.

This tradition was unique. I think anywhere else comes close. The best part was not just the tradition, but that the same people came year after year. We really were one big family. The group that came in February was a repeat crowd, but there were no children in that group. Only me, the littlest Feb.

The Lake Placid Club was like a small town inside a huge log building. It was built in rambling sections. The newest section was Agora - six floors of rooms and the large theatre / auditorium / dance floor. The theatre was used for Christmas and New Year's pageants, and in the summer, the club put on summer extravaganzas. Because we went to the St. Lawrence, I was only at the LPC a few times in the summer, but I remember it had millions of activities, and I am sure it was lots of fun. Some of the people who came for Christmas also spent their summers there. Many large families would take one of the many cottages, ranging from six- and seven-bedroom houses to actual one-bedroom cottages. Most had their own kitchens and living rooms. They were ideal for families spending their entire summer in the same cottage year after year.

When we arrived at the front door of the club, we would drive up a ramp under a large porte cochère to check in. The lobby had an enormous front desk with stairs behind it to the offices. The entire club was a giant Adirondack camp. To the right of the front desk was a hallway with a beauty shop, a barber and a doctor's office. To enter the rest of the club, one turned left from the desk and went down a long living room that took a bend to the right. It had huge floor-to-ceiling windows that just went on and on. After making a turn with the living room furniture on the left, there was a US Post office for Lake Placid Club, NY. All over the club there was green carpeting that had pine cones on it. And on all the china there were the same pines cones. The Adorondak Shop in Lake Placid still sells that pattern.

After the post office were some offices and then a small shop for the in-house photographer, a complete pharmacy that I loved because I charged lots of candy and hid it in the Christmas manger in the back of the stage. After that was Ruthie's Run Ski Shop, right across from where tea was served every day at 4:30 PM in front of a roaring fire. Past there, a big staircase went upstairs. Across from those stairs was the Adirondack Room, which was a swishy up-scale dining room/ nightclub. There was always a band and dancing, and Mom and Dad went there for dinner parties or drinking and dancing after dinner. Past this was a large gift shop, and down another hall was Razooks, which also had a store in the Breakers in Palm Beach. At the end of this long hallway was a huge game room for kids with pinball machines, pool tables, and ping-pong. Finally, at the end of the hall, was the room where we put our skates on in the winter. It was the tennis area in the summer. In the winter, the club flooded the tennis courts to make an amazing ice rink, with a hockey rink on one side. The rink was open at night and if we were not watching a movie in Agora or at a childrens dance there would be mobs of kids would be out on the skating rink under the lights. There were speakers on the light posts so there was usually Tyrolian music playing.

On the second floor, in the back of the clubhouse, overlooking the tennis courts/skating rink, was the enormous dining room, which was actually three different rooms. Across from the main entrance to the dining room were two libraries. One was just for children; the other, larger one, all of rich, dark wood, was substantial. Melvil Dewey, who created the Dewey Decimal System for libraries, was a member of the LPC at the end of the 1800s and used to spend a lot of time there. The library was his gift to the club, and it was kept in his memory.

The Lake Placid Club was full of daily and special activities, and life there was fun for every age. We all skied at the LPC's own ski hill, Mt. Whitney. This little ski hill was only for club members, and it was where we spent many winter days.

The main club is gone now. It burned to the ground after a series of owners were unable to make a go of it. It was too isolated from modern transportation, too cold and icy to be a good ski destination, and so massive that calling it a white elephant was an understatement.

Whether it was skiing at Mt. Whitney with all our friends, attending movie night, a dance in Agora, special holiday parties, or even just having afternoon tea in the drawing room in front of Ruthie's Run, LPC was a piece of heaven on earth, and those who enjoyed it will never forget it. I still pine for it. I am sure I always will.

Chapter 2
Additions and Subtractions:
The Island and Farmington

In the summers, my father, mother, and I lived on board their beautiful Sparkman and Stevens 52' yawl, Venture III. We moored her at the Clayton Yacht Club.

As I grew bigger, they wanted a place to turn loose a small child, and that is how Grindstone Island came into my life. When I was five, my parents bought McRea Point on Grindstone Island, part of the Thousand Islands in the St. Lawrence River between Canada and the U.S A. Grindstone Island was and is heaven on earth. Nothing compares to the emotional attachment I have for this incredibly beautiful place. Every summer of my life, and later, my son Nick's, has been spent there, and with a little luck I will be able to go there until I die. Then I shall be cremated and buried behind our house with the family dogs.

I just recently found the Venture III, and through the wonders of the internet have become fast friends with her new owner. She is beautifully restored, now named Bounty, and moored in San Francisco Bay. One day soon, I hope I can sail on her again.

When we first came to Grindstone, we had a French chef named Michel Dubois, who spent his winters as the maître' d at the Fountainbleau Hotel in Miami Beach. My mother, who never cooked in the first place, was adamant about refusing to cook on the boat, saying she was not going to be stuck in a hot galley while everyone else was up on deck enjoying themselves. Michel did all the cooking on the boat and later at McRea Point. He always called me Louisie, never quite getting Weezie and unwilling to give up Louise. He was French, after all.

One time, Michel fried up a black water snake in a big wok. The smell sent all of us running from the house. Not one of us would eat it with him. My mother even had him hang the wok out in the garage with the 1960 International Scout Dad had bought to drive around the island. The smell never left it, and eventually that old wok was taken to the dump. None of us could ever imagine why he wanted to eat the snake, except for the fact that he was French, which we thought explained everything.

§

On the island, Dad gave Michel gardening duties, as well, though this was not his thing. Michel decided he preferred life on board to life in the garden and left our family to work full time at the Fontenbleu. Years later, my father was in San Francisco at the Fairmont Hotel, and the maitre d' was none other than Michel. Alanna, my son Nick's new bride, says her uncle Mac tells stories about the two of them going down to Alexandria Bay, picking up girls, and bringing them back to the Venture. Obviously, we were not on board.

Our next cook/gardener was a man named Carl, who had been a cook at Ft. Drum the US Army base outside of Watertown. I don't think my parents liked anything he cooked, but he made amazing root beer. He was only with us for one or two summers. The amazing Cliff Doster followed him.

When my father interviewed Cliff for the job of cook, gardener, and handyman, he was given Cliff's banker as a reference. My father called the banker, who said, "Mr. Ford, I have no idea how much money you have, but Mr. Doster probably has more." Before working for us, Cliff had worked many years for a woman who had a summer home on Point Peninsula on Lake Ontario. When this woman died, she left all her money to Cliff. I don't think he ever touched a penny of it. I heard that when he died, it all went back to her family.

Cliff was part of our family for fourteen years. He never took a day off from April 15th until December 5th. We had the most beautiful flower and vegetable gardens on the St. Lawrence. Cliff, always perfectly turned out, cooked and served us three meals a day in our little house, which was so small you could practically have handed over the food from the kitchen. Cliff himself lived on sugared donuts, Roman Meal bread, coffee, and booze.

§

One night, after driving the Scout into the river (and on other occasions, as well, whenever he felt it needed to be said), he told my dad, "Mr. Ford, I don't drink. Never touched a drop in my life." He would then stagger off to bed. My parents didn't care, as he was always in the kitchen with breakfast ready first thing every morning. Dad used to try to get him to take a day off, but he refused. He smoked a corncob pipe, and at sunset, he would sit by his little house out back and smoke his pipe.

One family besides Michel called me Louisie. Aunt Bertha McRea's family, who owned the farm next to our place, called me Louisie for years because that was how Michel, who took me over to meet Aunt Bertha's two grand nieces, Bonnie and Cathy, introduced me. I became good friends with these little girls and with the Marks' children, who lived on the other side of the bay. I was the oldest girl; Fleur Marks was a year younger than I, and then Bonnie and Cathy, who were a year younger than she was. Fleur also had two brothers— Peter, who was three days younger than me, a real loner, and spent all his time fishing, and Pom, who was really a bit too young to hang around with us. And Lisa Hein's family built a house on the end of the next point over. Lisa was my age. We had a great little gaggle of girls. We spent our days swimming off my dock with my mother reading, smoking a cigarette, and drinking a screwdriver under one of the big oak trees while watching us. Dad built a diving board on the dock, and we were there almost every day.

If it rained, and Bonnie was at her Aunt Bertha's, we hung out on Aunt Bertha's sun porch, listened to music, and played cards. If Bonnie wasn't around (she didn't come for the entire summer like the rest of us), we went to Fleur's house to play board games or cards with her brothers. I tried to get invited to stay for lunch on those days. After lunch, the Marks kids all had to read. If I wasn't included and reading along with them afterward, I would sit outside their house on a big rock to the west, waiting for the reading hour to be over.

Once, when Connie and I were about six, she came up to visit from Rochester, and Michel took us rowing in the Venture's dinghy. We rowed across McRea Bay. I remember, as clear as if it were yesterday, that it was hysterically funny to tease poor Michel about his "fire hose". We would be in fits of giggles and just would not stop. I remember Michel trying to pretend he was not laughing. He just kept rowing faster and faster until we found ourselves halfway into Thurso Bay. Of course, this only egged us on. We were merciless. I suppose, since neither of us had any real contact with boys, other than Harry Sullivan and Chippy Weismiller from Indian Spring Lane, we had no idea what to do. Teasing Michel was a great way to get out some of our childhood insecurities and indulge in the silliness that little girls enjoy. We had a lot of that.

§

Summers at McRea Point were wonderful, and between Grindstone Island and the Lake Placid Club, my childhood was definitely more happy then not. School barely registered. Until I was twelve, my parents took me out of school for the months of February and March to go to Placid and Top Knotch in Stowe.

Things didn't really change much until my mother died of breast cancer in 1970, when I was fifteen. What do I say about that? There are legions of books written about the trauma of losing one's mother at a young age. I never felt that it somehow made me different, or special, or in need of special treatment. It was tragic, but that's life, and the one thing I did learn from it was to get on with it. Feeling sorry for myself more now than I did then, perhaps because I am now a mother myself. I think I felt sorrier for myself for not having brothers and sisters than I did for not having a mother after I was fifteen. I guess I don't let myself dream about what it might have been like to have a mother growing up, since my conscious mind knew it wasn't possible.

I remember some things about my mother's death more than others. For instance, her cousin Rosemary sobbed uncontrollably whenever we saw her. My father and I found this almost unbearable, so we distanced ourselves from her and Aunt Sadie. We coped okay, but not if someone opened raw wounds around us all the time. I also remember that I found it a great injustice when Rosemary got upset with me because I didn't continue my mother's tradition of taking her Aunt Sadie, now well into her 90's, out to lunch each week. I was fifteen and in school every day. Lunch?

But many things began to change. Life had become interesting for me, especially at the Island. At first, it seemed like everything would work out very much for the best, though I realize now this may have been more of a fantasy than a near-reality. By the time of my mother's death, I had adopted myself into a large island family called the Howard-Smiths, who had six kids, including a boy named Mark, my first boyfriend.

It seemed like the kids' wonderful mother, Junie, would rescue me, though I don't think she knew it. She came into my life in a big way the summer Mom died. At the same time I was hanging around with her kids, mostly Mark, she started "hanging around" with my newly widowed father. Doug Howard-Smith, Junie's first husband, had died in 1969, the summer before my mother. It seemed the perfect fit. Widow and widower were both summer residents at Grindstone, and I was an only child starved for a big family: What could go wrong? My hopes rose further when Dad and Junie even looked at houses in Rochester that fall for all of us to live in after they married.

But it was not to be. Junie was also seeing Wilson Foster in California, where the family lived in the winter. From what I heard, she asked her kids whom they would prefer for a stepfather. The longhaired boys chose Wilson over my arch-conservative father, and that apparently sealed the deal, because she married Wilson. This was very sad for me, but she has stayed my adopted mother to this day, and I am still a grateful, honorary member of her big family. She just celebrated her eightieth birthday, having survived three husbands and cancer. I'm lucky she was there that year after my mother died, for she filled a deep void.

§

That winter, back in Rochester, with Junie and her family in California, my father and I tried to carry on as best we could. On some levels, we were stars, but on others, we failed miserably. Neither of us cooked, so when we were home for dinner, many nights I had chocolate chip cookies and Coca-Cola. Dad would cook a Stouffer's mac and cheese - which I think was the first frozen dinner. We would sit together watching the CBS Evening news with Walter Cronkite, just as we had always done, eating our dinner on TV trays in the family room—except now the dinner was not exactly dinner. On Sunday and Thursday nights, the Country Club of Rochester had a roast beef buffet, and we never missed those nights. A few other nights during the week, we went to the Genesee Valley Club, where I ordered escargot and filet mignon every night.

§

The next summer, things started to change at a dizzying rate. On Derby Day, visiting the Houston Country Club, my father met a twenty-six-year-old redhead named Claire Cooney. She had huge breasts. She came to Grindstone for the Fourth of July weekend, and on July 8—my mother's birthday, incidentally, and not even a year after she died—my dad married Claire. They had gone off to Watertown, supposedly to buy groceries. They called Cliff from the

Clayton Yacht Club, told him they had gotten married, and asked him to have me on the dock to meet them when they got back to the island.

I didn't like Claire from the start, and I am quite sure she didn't like me. She was not at all nice to me. In fact, the day after they got married, she told me I had to clean her bathroom. I had never cleaned a bathroom in my entire life, and I sure as hell wasn't going to clean one for her. I never did get a chance to know her. Later that month, my father took her to Iceland to go salmon fishing. When they returned, her attitude toward me was even worse. To say we hated each other is probably an understatement. But that summer, while my father was away, many exciting things started to happen. He evidently thought that at sixteen, I was old enough to fend for myself and left me in the care of Cliff. At night, Cliff would go off with his regular drinking buddy, Francis Garnsey, the island mailman.

§

One night, I had all of my friends from nearby Juniper Island over. When Cliff returned, he grabbed his shotgun and told us he would shoot us if we didn't get out of the house immediately. We ran like hell for the end of the point. Once out there, of course, we had no idea what we should do next. Cliff sat on the front stoop of the tool shed, shotgun over his knees, smoking his pipe, and we couldn't get past him. For some reason, we decided to risk life and limb and pass Cliff to head for the swimming rocks in front of Aunt Bertha's house. Lisa Hien, who lived on the other side of the bay, had some pot, and we wanted to get it first, but to do that we had to get by the drunk caretaker. We did this by saying over and over, as I approached, "Cliff, it's me, Weezie. Don't shoot!" Cliff glared at us, but he let us pass.

Coming back that night, again we had to get by Cliff so the Rands could get back in their Boston whaler and go back to Juniper Island. He was still sitting on the stoop smoking his darned corncob pipe, his shotgun over his knee. Again, I said, "Cliff, it's me, Weezie. Don't shoot!"

We made it, or so we thought. Once we were all down on the dock, Cliff stood up and raised the shotgun. When we heard a click as he closed the previously broken gun, we all either dove into the water or the Rands' whaler. Cliff didn't shoot, however, and from what I can recall, just went off to bed. This is who my father left me alone with at the age of sixteen. Part of me wanted to ask, "Don't you give a shit?"

but the other part of me kept my mouth shut because I was thrilled to be on my own. I was having the time of my life.

The Rand family, who lived on Juniper Island, became important friends that summer and really my new family, with Junie remarried and staying in California with Wilson. Her kids only came up sporadically, except for Mark and Rick, who made a real effort to spend as much time on the island as possible. Rick pitched a tent, his mother having rented both of their houses, with his two big Scottish all these dogs in his single-engine Bonanza all the way from Palo Alto, camping next to the plane en route. Mark, much like me, had himself adopted into the already large Juniper Island family, and we had great times. Juniper is just the other side of Leek Island from my house, on the Canadian side, but somehow, I had never even seen the kids before that summer.

My best friend on Grindstone Island was Fleur Marks. A couple of girls my age from Rochester, Sarah Castle and Lili Ward, stayed on Punts Island that summer. The four of us got into my little thirteen foot Boston Whaler and went to Gananoque on the Canadian side to the Wednesday night dance at the Canoe Club. We really thought we were something else to be able to do this, since it meant going out on the river, at night, something our parents would never have let us do earlier and they didn't do themselves. With my father away, I did whatever I wanted.

§

One fateful night at a Canoe Club dance, the four of us were standing on the balcony looking down at the docks when a "big" (sixteen-foot) Boston whaler pulled into the dock carrying what we thought were the dreamiest, hunkiest, long-haired boys we had ever seen. It was the Rand boys—Doug, Jeff, and Chip—who all had long, curly blond hair. Doug, I later learned, always wore a ponytail because his curls were so wild that was the only way to contain his hair. The oldest brother, he had a full beard, too. Jeff, the middle brother, had light brown hair down to the middle of his back—also curly, but not wild like Doug's. Chip, the youngest brother, had the most beautiful blond long mane, and blue eyes to go with it. Their sister Lyn, strawberry blond curls, who was my age, was there as well. As if the Rand boys were not enough, Doug had three friends from Princeton, New Jersey, with him. Rob Scanlon, who was almost albino, had long, straight white hair. Steve Paice had long, dark brown curls, and last, but not least, there was Ricky Lohman—who was black and had a big afro. In 1971, we thought we had died and gone to heaven, just to see these Delphic dudes (as my friend Katy Keiffer would later dub them).

So here we were, these giggly teenage girls, standing upstairs on the balcony of the Canoe Club with our mouths hanging open, when Fleur starts screaming, "They're from Princeton. They're from Princeton! Oh, my God!" Fleur was from Princeton, too. Well, that was all it took. It turned out that Rob Scanlon's sister was in Fleur's class at Princeton High School. The connection was made.

We had a blast. We got the cutest, coolest guys we had ever seen to dance with. That night changed my life forever. When the dance ended, we all went down to the dock, and the Rand gang got jealous because my thirteen-foot whaler had a 40 hp outboard on it—the same as their sixteen-foot whaler. Doug said, "Come over tomorrow so we can water ski behind your boat. It'll get us up out of the water much better." So the next day I did, and I kept it up almost every day that summer and for many more summers, long after I was married and had my son and their wonderful mother had died.

The Rand kids were the fifth generation on Juniper Island, which was owned by their mother, Patty Bain, who had inherited it with her brother Bud in the 1960s, when their father died. Shortly after, Patty bought out her brother's share. The seven-acre island was bought and built on in the early 1900s by the Sargent family from New York City. The main cabin looks like a large Adirondack camp with bark-covered logs on the outside. It sits in the middle of the island with a long lawn that goes down to, flat pink granite rocks that slope gently into the water. The rocks are wonderful for swimming, like being on a beach sloping into the water—but none of the nasty sand.

It has a large living room with a river stone fireplace, a dining room with three sides of small-paned glass windows, a billiards room, and a very large kitchen and pantry. On the back of the main cabin is a big, screened-in porch, with old implements, insulators, tools, and other objects from around the island hanging from the walls and ceilings. There is a big wooden table, making it the perfect place for breakfast.

The front of the main cabin has a long, large, open front porch with a roof held up by what once were trees. It's furnished with old wicker furniture. The view across the lawn, under the trees and down to the river is wonderful. On a beautiful evening or night, it is a great place to hang out and watch the lightning from a summer thunderstorm.

The main cabin was designed for socializing. There are no bedrooms. At the end of the point, facing southwest, is the Point cabin, which was Patty's cabin, just as it had been her father's before her. At the foot of Juniper Island, high up on a cliff overlooking the bay, where the boathouse is, is the guest cabin. It has two bedrooms, a bathroom, and big living room with a huge, old bear rug.

There are also two smaller sleeping cabins, built for Patty and her brother when they were kids and not as grand as the other two. In the early 1970s, these were the boys' and girls' cabins, though the only girl was sister Lyn. Finally, Juniper Island had a large, rather famous boathouse, designed by Tiffany's architectural department in 1911. Over the boat house there are five bedrooms, a living room, and kitchen, built to house the servants.

Patty had just recently married her third husband, David Bain, who was Canadian and lived in Toronto. She had moved her family up there from Princeton. Because they were newlyweds, Patty went back to Toronto during the week with David and left all the kids on the island with just the help. They had a Jamaican maid named Peggy who became part of the gang, smoking pot right along with us. She had amazing fingernails and she loved wash our hair down by the river. Peggy was tasked with looking after Patty's youngest son, Price, from her second marriage. Price is ten years younger than I am, so in 1971, my first summer on Juniper, he was six.

We celebrated a succession of Summers of Love on Juniper, just a little later than the rest of the world. It was one party after another. We spent the days skinny-dipping and sunbathing on the rocks and waterskiing. Doug and my friend Sarah Castle started going out together that first summer. One weekend, when her parents were going back to Rochester for the week, Sarah wanted to stay up on the river so she could be with Doug. She called her parents and put Doug on the line, saying he was David Bain. Doug, who always had a very deep voice, told them, "Patty and I would just love to have Sarah and Lili spend the week on Juniper with us." Her parents fell for it, and Sarah and Lili stayed on Juniper for the week.

The boys built a helmet meant to help us get even more stoned. It was made out of a black plastic bag and coat hangers and we put it over our heads. Someone blew pot smoke into the helmet, and we were supposed to just breathe it in. I never liked the feeling I got when smoking pot, so I only tried a couple of times, but it was fun watching everyone else. Best of all was Ricky Lohman, with his big Afro. He would come out from under the helmet with his hair full of smoke. If you patted him on the head, the smoke rose like Indian smoke signals.

That week with Sarah and Lili was so much fun we forgot all about her parents returning. One day, when Ricky had the helmet on his head, sitting on the pool table with the music blasting, Sarah and Lili's parents walked by the window. We all screamed and scrambled for cover. I was sent out on the front porch because I knew the Castles from Rochester.

Somehow, the girls got away with Sarah's parents none the wiser that there were no adults anywhere. They had arrived with a big basket full of thank-you presents for the Bains. We had no idea what to do with them, so we put them in the attic under some old boxes. Years later, Patty was up there looking for something and came down the stairs with this wonderful, untouched basket saying, "Look at this! Where did this come from?" We were all in hysterics.

§

At the end of August 1971, I told my father I wasn't looking to drop out of school, but there was no way I could live with the new wife. Dad asked if I would consider boarding school, and I said, "Sure, I guess so. Why not? Anything was better than having to live with Claire." So on Labor Day weekend, Dad and I climbed into the car and went looking at boarding schools. Forget the fact that they were all starting in the next week, and the admission process usually took months.

Our whirlwind tour started with Emma Willard in Albany, Miss Hall's in western Massachusetts, and Miss Porter's in Farmington, Connecticut. Since school wasn't yet in session in any of them, I had no idea what the girls in these schools were like. Somehow, Dad managed to get me into all three schools. Anyway, I picked Miss Porter's because I loved the New England campus.

When Dad and I arrived home to Rochester, Claire was in New York City. Marie helped me pack my bags, and I was put back on a plane just a couple of days later. I went feeling very cool on the one hand, particularly now that I had a bunch of friends like the Rands, but I was also terrified. Would I fit in? I was very much on my own at just sixteen, and Dad had sent me off to this new school all by myself. The dreadful part of this story is that within one week of my going away to school, Claire left him, lock, stock, and barrel. She took many of my mother's things with her, Marie, who was disgusted by the whole mess, later told me.

Dad had the marriage annulled. He didn't tell me what had happened until Parents' Weekend at Miss Porter's, sometime in October or early November. Dad told me Claire had a smart Jewish lawyer, but he had a smarter one. So there I was in boarding school, not really ever wanting to go there, and now the reason I had gone didn't exist. That weekend, Dad booked himself a room in Avon Old Farms—not at the Farmington Inn, where everybody else's parents stayed. He had done this, he told me, so that Claire's lawyers couldn't find him. He spent the entire winter living on our 35' Magnum, which he had shipped from the island down to Palm Beach. He was booked into marinas as George Ward, instead of George Ford. He had to pay off about twenty-five thousand dollars of Claire's bills, but he felt he had gotten off easy. I guess he did, in dollars and cents, but for me, the price was a huge change in my life.

My year at Miss Porter's was mixed. I loved my new friends, and some of them are still my best friends. I didn't give a damn about my studies, but then I had never been much of a student. I wasn't flunking out; I was just not a shining star. For the most part, my memories of the place are very good because of my friends. That is not to say we were not often bored to tears. We played endless games of cards, like Spike Malice, and once we played Parcheesi all weekend long. Nights after dinner, a couple of us ordered pizza from the local delivery place. It was the best pizza in the entire world. I can taste it even now. It had the greasiest, most delicious cheese. I've never had pizza as good.

Interestingly, the school let us smoke if we had parental permission. In my case, this was no problem, since I had started smoking in front of my father about a month after my mother died. Sitting in the Pierre in New York City, age fifteen, I told him I wasn't going to hide in the bushes any longer. All the MPS girls I meet up with nowadays remember the smoking room a horrible, dirt floored basement under Main, the administration building. The air in the damp cellar was pungent from all the smoke. It was cold because we kept the door to the outside open all the time; it was all the air we got. Juliana used to come down wearing a scarf around her head to keep the smoke from stinking up her hair. I have no idea why she bothered since there wasn't a boy around for a million miles who might possibly smell her hair.

There was a townie named Willie with a long ponytail that rode a motorbike—not even a motorcycle, I don't think. I have no idea what he did or how we knew his name was Willie. Anyway, we would lie on Juliana's bed looking out her window at the stoplight in front of our dorm, and lo and behold, Willie would ride by. If we were lucky, he would have to stop at the light, and we could oohh and ahhh at him while he sat there. I wonder if he had any idea that he was our fantasy man.

§

The year went along pretty well. I got into the groove of school, and with all my new friends, I was pretty happy. Dad and I spent our last Christmas at the Lake Placid Club. It had become a hotel and completely changed. Most of the old club members just stopped coming. Around the same time, the ski areas in Colorado were really taking off. It was much easier to fly to Denver from New York City than drive up to Lake Placid. It was the perfect storm, and it killed the place. That last Christmas, Liz Hager, who was also at MPS, was there with her family, and we became fast friends. Her family also had a place in the Thousand Islands. Her grandfather, Bronson Quackenbush, had invented the nutcracker, and Liz's friends learned to check all nutcrackers for the Quackenbush logo. For spring break, Dad took Liz Hager, Sandy Teall, and me to Lake Tahoe skiing, Mark Howard-Smith took the bus up from their home in Atherton, CA to ski with us. We then went to San Francisco for a few days afterwards.

For Memorial Day weekend, I met Dad in Florida. He had finally rented an apartment in Old Port Cove, where he could keep the Magnum at the docks there. On that trip, we bought our first house down there. Dad liked a couple of houses—one on Lake Worth, and another on the golf course. I was adamant that if you were going to live in Florida, you should live on the beach, so he bought a place on the ocean in the Lost Tree Club, 11572 Turtle Beach Road.

§

At the end of the school year at Miss Porter's, my class, the juniors, were given lottery numbers to pick rooms and roommates for senior year. I got a very low number and was able to get a single room in one of the two senior dorms. School was off for Memorial Day weekend, and we were due back to take our finals before we were free on summer vacation. Just as I was leaving to fly to Palm Beach for the weekend, Headmaster Dick Davis called me to his office to tell me that I was not being asked back next year because "I had a bad attitude." I was stunned. They had just let me pick out my room for the next year. I was NOT flunking out. What was going on? My father found out as I was en route to Florida. Dick Davis called him. Dad was livid.

Oddly, no one seemed to feel that having just lost my mother and being driven from home by a hideous stepmother might be enough to give me a "bad attitude". Which I don't think in my entire life I have ever actually had something that could be called a "bad attitude"! Only much later did I find out that a girl named Molly Schuler, whose father had gone to Harvard with Dick Davis, had told the headmaster that she didn't like me, that I wasn't the right type of girl for MPS, and that I should leave.

One wonderful history teacher went to bat for me that last week, while I was struggling through my exams, but no one else gave a damn. I remember taking one multiple-choice test and just playing tic-tac-toe with the little dots. I am sure my final grades only reinforced Dick Davis's feeling that he had done the right thing.

Oh, well, I thought. Claire was gone. I could go home and be with my dad, which made me happy. Sort of. The best part of senior year back home for me was that the boys' school in Rochester had merged with the girls' school I had gone to since seventh grade, after leaving Sacred Heart because they were closing the Rochester School, so I went back that year to a brand new, coed school—now called the Allendale Columbia school. Before that, I had another idyllic summer on Grindstone Island, spending most of my time hanging out on Juniper Island and having all the adventures and misadventures of a carefree youth in paradise. This summer, Doug dated Fleur, which was really fun for me.

I don't remember feeling deprived at having lost my mother, though of course, I missed her. I remember telling my friends at Miss Porter's one day about her death. It was just a year later, yet I was able to talk about it as if it were simply a fact of life. I was astonished, and remember to this day, that my friend Katy Keiffer started crying when she heard the story. I was surprised by her reaction. I didn't understand what made Katy cry. I think I understand now, but at the time, my mother's death was just a fact. I was coping as best I could.

My father got on with his life, and that is exactly what I did, following his lead. We carried on. Maybe his Scotch/English upbringing helped. I'm sure how he dealt with it had to do with losing his own parents when he was just a wee bairn, younger than I was when I lost Mom. I have to thank him for that. In many ways, the experience made me tough and more able to enjoy my life. Today, I would be expected to talk about my loss and feel sorry for myself.

Meanwhile, my father was mortified by the mistake he made in marrying Claire. I don't think he ever recovered from the poor judgment he showed. He continued to date extensively, as I think all "rich" widowers do when they are let loose into an enormous population of desperate widows—what women become after their lives as desperate housewives—but Dad certainly slowed down after the Claire debacle.

Chapter 3
Two Marriages:
Palm Beach to Points Elsewhere and Back

During my senior year, Dad was living in Rochester and had the house in Florida. While in Rochester, he was often off shooting, fishing, or whatever and when he was away, Marie and Frank stayed in the house to take care of me. Until I gave that big, out-of-control party, and she said she wasn't willing to keep on with this duty. Dad just said okay and left me on my own after that.

A turn of events was about to make a huge change in my father's life—and my own—though I didn't know it. My father brought a "date" to my graduation from Allandale Columbia. When I was a senior, my father hired Burdines department store to furnish the Lost Tree house. They sent over their in-house decorator, a Colombian woman named Beatriz Algarra. Bea told Dad she was thirty years his junior. In fact, she was only twenty years younger. Also, her birthday, which was always celebrated by us on March 18, turned out to be May 18. Lying about one's age I can understand—but lying about what time of year it was? This is just one of the many things that became known after Dad was gone.

Bea never explained to my father or myself why her entire family (three brothers, one sister, and their mother) left Colombia and moved to Long Island. We never heard about her father. Eventually the family ended up in South Florida. (Her sister now works at a Burdines in Tampa, and her youngest brother is at Office Depot in Boca Raton.)

Dad dated Bea for about a year, though he saw other women as well. He dated a Russian princess who worked in the fur department at Lord & Taylor in NYC. She made him buy me my first fur coat. He also dated a Miss Iceland for a while. We didn't go anywhere without women chasing after my father. One French girl at Lake Placid ended up teaching Bea and I French in Palm Beach years later. Until she told me who she was, I didn't remember. Bea never liked her. I think she found out she was one of Dad's old girlfriends.

§

Christmas 1973, my dad invited Bea to spend the holiday skiing with us at Lake Tahoe, but she never showed up. He was obviously distressed by this. He asked me then if I thought she would make a good wife. I told him that since she was Catholic, she probably would. My mother had been a devout Catholic, and I assumed at the time all Catholics were honest and down-to-earth, since that's how my mother had been. I was nineteen—what did I know?

Bea told me later that she didn't know how to ski and was not interested in learning how, although she told Dad at the time she was. She used to pull back just when she was expected to be around. On February 16, 1974, less than two months later, they were married.

There was no doubt that my father found Bea sexy and exciting. With her Colombian accent, she was a cross between Charo and Eva Gabor with black hair. Mom had been salt-of-the-earth, no-nonsense, well bred, classic looking, and perfectly natural. My father, whose life with my mother had been mostly sexless (they had separate bedrooms), was bowled over by this racy, sexy woman whose imperfect English was part of her flirting. "Oh , Yorge, what is a touch down? It sounds so sexy!" was one of her regular lines. Dad was attracted in the way only men who have had good, but probably boring marriages can be.

Bea introduced him to the international scene in NYC; one night at a dinner party, Dad sat next to what he thought was a nice Italian woman. Afterwards, Bea asked him if he had enjoyed talking to Gina. Dad said, "Oh, is that her name?" She was Gina Lollobrigida. Dear old Dad had no idea.

Bea arrived in the marriage without a dime to her name. She, her mother, and her brother Fernando lived in a tiny rented house at the north end of Palm Beach owned by Bill Brooks. (He at the time coincidentally worked for my Uncle Mort, then executive Vice President of Scripps Howard Broadcasting, which owned Channel 5 in Palm Beach. Bill told me many times what awful tenants they were— he was thrilled when Bea married my father, because now her mother's rent was paid on time.) Dad Later bought her mother a house in Coral Gables.

Bea drove an old, sage green Pontiac, one of those long ones with two doors and a fabric roof, one step away from the red bombshell on the Dukes of Hazzard. Within weeks of returning from their honeymoon at Las Brisas in Acapulco, Bea was driving a gorgeous, brand new, baby blue 500 Mercedes with a white leather interior.

They were married in her little rented house in Palm Beach. This house was so small that the ceremony took place in an area that was both entrance hall and living room. Bea and her mother shared a bedroom, and Fernando had a room behind the garage. Besides the bride and groom and justice of the peace, there were only three other people there—Fernando, who was Dad's best man, Bea's closest friend, the gossip columnist on the Palm Beach Shiny Sheet, and me as a second bridesmaid. She had me wear a hideous brown chiffon dress, in spite of the fact that there were six people there. This never made any sense to me. There was no announcement in the papers. They didn't get married in a church. It seemed odd for a woman who craved the social spotlight when she was marrying the millionaire of her dreams. (When I got married, Bea had a friend of hers put my wedding in Town and Country Magazine. Why didn't she do this with hers?)

At first, I was happy Dad married someone who seemed nice and would make him happy. He certainly was taken with her, and that was important to me. During the early years of their marriage, I was living on my own in Colorado and then London, and Dad having a nice life made mine easier in a way. Two years after Dad and Bea married, they threw a big party at the Sailfish Club in Palm Beach for their anniversary. It was a big party, but very private, and I remember Bea always saying it was terrible to have anything in the social pages. Again, that made no sense to me at all because she usually loved to appear in the Shiny Sheet. By this time, I understood that climbing the society ladder was her real aim in life.

Dad gave Bea a huge Colombian emerald and diamond ring as an engagement ring and a diamond band just like my mother's for a wedding ring. For a wedding present, he gave her a pair of emerald and diamond earrings. (She would manage to lose one on the airplane to Mexico. They had everyone in First Class on their hands and knees looking for it until it was found.)

Later there was a private party at the Royal Poinciana Club. This club was in the Royal Poinciana shopping mall and it was sort of a glorified eating club. A lot of strangeness enters the story here: This, we were told was Bea's first marriage - then almost forty-seven years old. She lied about her age, telling Dad she was thirty-eight when they got married when she was almost 47. There was no announcement in the local papers, and the only record of their getting married is the marriage certificate which shows Bea's Birthday as March 18. You also can clearly see where the birthday has had "white out" used on the original in the Palm Beach County Court House. In reality, her baptism certificate, driver's license and Colombian Cedula (citizenship papers issued a year after my father died, 2007, also odd, normally issued at the age of 18 or in Bea's case 1946!) give her date of birth as May 18.

For the thirty years she was married to my father, Bea celebrated her birthday in March, making a very big deal about being a Pisces. She even bought a large double Pisces fish and placed it in the middle of the living room.

§

Right after Dad and Bea were married, I stopped going to classes at college. I had moved in January 1974 up to Evergreen, Colorado with a few friends, including Lyn Rand from Juniper Island. Megan Kuntze, my new best friend from DU (University of Denver), rented a house just down the street with her old friends Peter Croto and Meg Canavan, whom she knew from summering on Lake George. Peter came out of the closet that year. Before this, I had a terrible crush on him and couldn't understand why he was so uninterested, even though we hung out together all the time. Megan and I were in Florida and sitting at the bar at the Lost Tree Club when she told me he was gay. Talk about being hit by a ton of bricks. I had never known anyone that was gay, but now I did, and it was Peter, on whom I had this big crush. That was the end of my romantic hopes. Peter died of AIDS just before the effective three-drug cocktail was introduced. The three of us were best friends until we lost him.

The following winter, Peter Croto and I shared a condo in Breckenridge, Colorado, on the mountain across from the ten-mile range. My first job was slopping chili on top of hot dogs at the restaurant on top of Peak 9. I lasted about a month at this seven- day-a-week job, which gave me a ski pass, but never any time off to ski. After a month, I asked if I could have a day off, and when the manager said no, I quit. The ski pass stayed good for the entire season, and I moved on to a job as cocktail waitress in a very busy, hip little bar called the Angel's Rest. The owner was Ray Romero, who though he was fifty-one and I was just twenty, made a big play for me. He was still quite attractive and in the uninhibited atmosphere that we lived in then, I thought it was kind of fun. Ray had a Porsche 911, which he gave me to drive, and a Cessna 182. He took me to Mexico for two months in the Cessna. I learned to fly his plane, and we flew up and down the Baja and the entire west coast of Mexico. It was a lark for me, but not for him, as he took our relationship very seriously. The next fall, I moved to Aspen with Doug, Jeff, and Lyn Rand, and Ray followed. He wanted to marry me. The entire concept was just not imaginable to me, and I broke up with him, but he sort of stalked me. He came to the house, ostensibly to see the Rands, and then hid in my closet and jumped out when I came into the room. He and Lyn Rand managed to get together and she ended up staying with him for eleven years. Her mother, Patty, told me many times that she could kill me for introducing Lyn to him. I told her I had nothing to do with Lyn's choice.

§

During the winter in Aspen, Peter Croto and his boyfriend, and Charlie Shields and his best friend stayed in our living room. Both of them were there for a long time, and it was a great happy house. It turned out the owners were divorcing, and it was on the market for $98,000—a three-bedroom in Old Snowmass. I begged my father to buy it for me, but he said it was too much money. Oh, if only he had bought it, what a nest egg that would have been for me, the anchor that I never did seem to be able to put down for very long. I always wonder if I had been able to buy the house how different my life would have been.

The following three winters, I went to live in London, coming back each summer to stay on Grindstone. At first, I lived with Robert and D.D. Buxton at The Brook House, Pembroke Road in Kensington, and then I rented a flat at 49 Redcliff Road off the Fulham Rd. London was swinging then and lots of fun. My main boyfriend was Simon Ortiz-Patino, D.D. Buxton's son and heir to the Patino Bolivian tin fortune. Unfortunately, his father and stepmother in Geneva didn't want anything to do with him, so I ended up paying for everything. Simon always promised that he would pay me back when he inherited. He never did. Live and learn. We lived in hotels, went to club openings, and drank nothing but Dom Perignon. His mother and Step father

Robert and DD are still very much my original, much loved, London family.

Whenever Simon and I were going through bad patches—and there were quite a few - I went out with George Rodney, who was the 11th Lord Rodney. George sadly passed away earlier this year. George's sister Ann is still one of my very best friends. Their ancestor, Admiral Lord Rodney, invented the battleship technique that Nelson used at Trafalgar, called "breaking the line" -with the result that Lord Rodney, more famous originally than Nelson, faded into the background. This turned out to be one of life's weird coincidences. I now live in a house that was part of Admiral Rodney's estate, the original house owned until eight years ago by my partner, Peter McDermott. The admiral and all eleven subsequent Lord Rodney's are buried in the churchyard next door, including George and Ann's parents, whom I knew very well. And now sadly my old friend George. Right before meeting Peter, I went to the funeral of their mother, Regine. I remember Ann saying that afterward they were going down to some little church in Hampshire where all the Rodneys were buried. Small world.

§

I left London eventually because I had to leave Simon. The situation with him was very unhealthy. I first went out to California and stayed with Junie Howard-Smith Foster and her kids for about a month. Then I went back to Palm Beach. After only a few weeks, I met Wayne Grant at Marrakech, the bar the Palm Beach "in" crowd all hung out in every night. He told me I had a great ass and asked whether I would like to join his harem. I, of course, told him to "F off," but within a week, we were going out. A few weeks later, we drove to New York City, where he had a job on Wall Street lined up. After a couple of days, that was history, and he and I took off for Grindstone Island. We spent the next winter in San Francisco. I worked for EF Hutton as a sales assistant for eleven brokers, and Wayne was a waiter in a restaurant called the Sailing Ship. Dolph Remp, whose father started Adolph's Meat Tenderizer business, owned the restaurant. That is where we met Jock McLean, who turned out to live within eyeshot of us on Grindstone.

Dad and Bea visited us in San Francisco on their way to skiing at Lake Tahoe; Bea was still pretending to like skiing. We spent our first day showing them around the city. Dad had been there but Bea never had. She couldn't have cared less about the sights. She spent the entire day acting like a spoiled child, saying, "Jeeeorrgggge, I want to go to Gumps!" Finally, we went to Gumps. Dad, Wayne, and I walked around this dark store looking at all the Chinese stuff and shaking our heads. What a waste of time, but it was what Bea wanted, and she got it. When we were up at Lake Tahoe sometime after that, Bea claimed she had hurt her foot and that she couldn't get into her new ski boots because of it. Bea never did ski with us.

Riding up the chair lift at Alpine Meadows one day with Dad, I told him that Wayne and I were going to get married. I wanted a baby, and I had told Wayne that either he was going to be the father or I would find someone else. My biological clock was in overdrive. I asked Dad if I could have Mom's diamond engagement ring. He told me he didn't have it. It was stolen off Mom's finger, he said, in the hospital. I was never sure I believed this, because I wouldn't have put it past him to have traded Mom's ring for Bea's emerald. I will never know.

Within two years of marrying him, Bea had talked Dad out of the house on the beach at Lost Tree and into the house at 300 Regent Park, Palm Beach. Her grand ambition was to be the next queen of Palm Beach, a title held in those days by Mary Sanford. Bea even went so far as to hire Mary Sanford's cook Manolo, trying to be just like her. Dad paid $500k for the house, which was fairly new and had a long lawn going down to the shore of Lake Worth and practically across the street from the Bath and Tennis Club. I recently uncovered legal documents that show that at the end of Dad's life, when he was very old and frail, Bea wrote a lawyer asking for the names on the deed to be changed. I have attached it at the end of this book. Originally, the house was in trust for Bea to live in for the rest of her life, and it would come back to me upon her death. In one of the FIVE changed in the last four years of his life, Dad left the house outright to Bea. Dad was almost 98 yrs old when he died.

By this time, Bea had a well-established routine to get my father to give her what she wanted. Dad was a self-made man who had lived through the Depression and two World Wars. He was not interested in parties or being part of society, but Bea was—and still is. He put up with the Palm Beach scene, and in return, he led the life of an outdoor sports enthusiast, which is where his heart remained.

§

In 1978, Bea announced her refusal to go to Dad's much-loved house on Grindstone Island. She hated the place and swore that she would never again set foot on that awful island. She said Dad should sell the place and move to Newport, Rhode Island, for the summer so that she could be part of the seasons in both Newport and Palm Beach. (This is exactly how she phrased it.) It took her many years to get him to Newport. He fought it because he despised the idea and always hated the place.

This development turned out to be a great thing for me, because in 1979, I took over running the house on Grindstone Island. That first summer, I was very lucky that Wayne had decided to run off there with me, as I certainly needed his help. We put in a huge vegetable garden and found that running the place without help was a full-time job. No complaints—we loved it. That summer, we had our pet pig, Arnold, and in San Francisco, right before we left, we got Boo, a four-week-old pit bull—the most loving, wonderful, smart, athletic dog I have ever seen. She would climb stepladders and run around on people's roofs. She water-skied and windsurfed with Wayne. She would dive under the water, bring up rocks from the bottom, and chew on them. When she died at the age of fifteen, our son Nicky went to get a rock out of the river to put in the grave with her. Boo was such a great dog that she converted many of our friends to pit bull ownership.

After Bea made him give up going to Grindstone Island, Dad bought a salmon camp in the Gaspe Peninsula on the Quebec/New Brunswick border. This place made Grindstone Island look like a social epicenter. The only neighbors were drunken Indians on welfare. Dad went there for seven years until Bea once again put her foot down, refused to go anymore, and repeatedly cried, "I want to go to Newport!"

§

Wayne and I were married on November 28, 1980, in St. Edward's Catholic Church in Palm Beach. We had our reception at the Bath & Tennis Club. The wedding was at seven PM, and it was "black tie." Lester Lanin's orchestra played. The place was packed with people Bea was using to social-climb as well as a few that were old friends of Dad's, Wayne's family, and mine. I think there were a couple of hundred people there. About a month before the actual wedding, Dad got cold feet about paying for it. He offered to let me have it in the back garden at 300 Regent Park, but Bea was adamant that it be at the club. Bea really made him push the boat out for this, and I was always grateful to her for that. She made sure I got the dress I wanted, even though Dad said it cost too much. The wedding was beautiful, and we had an enormous cake. Towering high over our heads and the photo Wayne and I cutting the cake was in Town & Country. It was a very rainy day, and on the way to the church in the limo, just as we were about to arrive, Dad announced that he need to find a bathroom ! The driver was very resourceful and took us down one of the ocean blocks to a condo on the ocean. Dad ran in, and the doorman gave him a place to go. In the meantime, all these people were coming and going from this building, looking into the back of the car and pointing, saying things like, "Look, it's a bride!"

My one enduring memory of my wedding was standing at the altar, repeating my vows, and wondering why I didn't seem to be feeling any of it. Why? I was marrying a very handsome man. Only years later did I realize I wanted the dream, the whole Prince Charming thing, so much that I was willing to overlook and even forget all the stuff that was wrong between Wayne and me. The problems had been obvious before we married, but I guess I justified it for whatever reason women do these things.

Wayne was a cocaine user when we met. I had experimented with different drugs because they were always around, but I never really liked them. I had never liked smoking pot because it made me feel weird and paranoid. "Heavier" drugs also tended to freak me out, but doing coke and dancing all night seemed like a lot of fun. I should have seen, however, that this was a serious addiction. On my twenty-fifth birthday in San Francisco, we had a particularly wild night of champagne and coke. We were with many of our good West Coast friends, but at some point, Wayne and I ended up outside the restaurant, we were fighting, I have no idea about what, and he beat me up rather badly. I was black and blue for days. I should have run for the hills, but I didn't. He never did hit me again but he sadly used violence more than once with our son.

I also naively thought that once we were married and "settled down," Wayne would do just that, but that was not the way it went. The first winter we were married we were living in Palm Beach, and saying it was a wild time would be an understatement. At some point, around March, I just stopped doing coke. I had had enough. I wasn't able to think clearly anymore, and to this day, I think my brain has a lot of holes from what I did to it in those days. Also, I wanted to get pregnant, which was really the driving force for my getting married.

§

In June 1981, while staying on a friend's sailboat in Annapolis, Maryland, Wayne's hometown, our son Nick was conceived. A few weeks later, I realized I was pregnant and immediately stopped drinking. Finding out I was going to have a baby was one of the happiest days of my life. I remember telling Wayne that the test stick was positive and crying tears of joy.

While we were on Grindstone Island, the coke use was minimal, if at all. It's important to remember that in the 1970's and '80s, coke was everywhere. Time magazine put cocaine on its cover and said that it was not addictive.

§

Once we returned to Palm Beach in the fall, regardless of my pregnancy, Wayne got right back into the coke use. I did the only thing I knew how to do—move. We moved up to South Salem, New York, to be near my cousin Rosemary in Connecticut. She had four kids by then, and I knew that she was the ideal family member to help me with what I was about to go through. Her husband Eddie's friend owned a booming business right on the NY/CT border. At that time, there were heavy taxes in CT on beer, but not in NY State. Wayne got a job as a manager of Barney's Beer Barn in Vista, NY. It did incredible business. Most of the state of CT came there to buy their beer. It was only a big warehouse, and people came by the hundreds every day to fill their cars and go back to Bridgeport of Greenwich, or as far away as New Haven. It was a good job for Wayne, and he made good money at it. We lived there for two and half years, and for that time, Wayne was mostly cocaine-free. I learned later that this is known as a geographic cure, not a real cure, but for the time being, it worked out very well for all concerned.

I had a normal pregnancy, except I let myself gain fifty pounds and was the size of a house. The baby was late. I wasn't dilating, and the Doctors waited without doing anything until I was three weeks late. For some reason, the doctor had told me that the baby would probably be early. I woke every morning for the last two months and asked why nothing had changed, fully expecting that when I went to sleep at night I would wake up in labor. When I woke without any change, it was awful.

To make matters worse, my poor father was sitting in Palm Beach with a plane ticket, waiting. He called every day, asking, "What's going on?"

"Oh, I don't know, Dad. This kid has decided to move in permanently. No plans to move out and get his own place."

Finally, on the morning of March 31, Wayne and I went to White Plains Hospital to meet the doctor and have him induce labor. My due date had been March 5. The doctor broke my water using something that looked like a crochet hook. I immediately went into hard labor. I spent twelve hours in something called "transition labor." It was supposed to only last about an hour at the very end of the ordeal, but mine never ended. I only dilated to four centimeters, and nothing my body could do would make me dilate any more.

Early on in the experience I had fired Wayne as my coach. As hard as he must have tried, he could not help me. The pain was severe. The monitor showed that when I came down off one contraction, before the meter even reached the bottom, it would shoot back up again, and I would have another contraction. One right on top of the other. No breaks. They let me go on like this for 12 hours. Someone finally realized that I was dying and sent for the doctor.

Wayne stayed outside the operating room watching through a window in the door. I looked up and saw a Chinese man, the anesthesiologist. He had his syringe ready to go, and I said, "Just do it. What are you waiting for?"

He said he had to wait until the doctors showed up. Off to my right I saw the two doctors scrubbing up and talking about a game of golf they'd played in Israel. I screamed something to the effect of "Knock it off and get in here. Hurry up! I don't give a damn about your golf game or trip to Israel! Hurry up! I don't want an April Fool's baby!" Eventually, they knocked me out.

The rest I know from Wayne, who watched the whole thing through the window. They opened me up. There was tons of blood. Nicky was pulled out, and he immediately started crying and peeing on the nurses. I was taken to recovery, where I woke up with a nurse standing over me holding this little papoose wrapped tightly in a blue blanket saying, "It's a boy. It's a boy!" I was too knocked out to talk, but I remember thinking, "I know it's a boy. I always knew it was a boy. Please do not put him on my stomach."

We didn't even have any serious girls' names because I was sure that the little creature inside me was a boy. At 11:45 PM, March 31, 1982, Nicholas George Grant was born.

Sometime in the middle of the night, they wheeled me into my hospital room and we passed the nursery. On the way they brought Nicky, all wrapped up in his little bundle and put him up next to my face on my right shoulder—my stomach was still in no condition to have anything put on it. The old cliche is true: at the moment I saw that little tiny face right next to mine and I fell madly in love.

§

The next morning, I woke up to find blood dripping into my arm. I was in the midst of being given two pints of blood because my blood loss in the operating room had been so severe. They had gone in very quickly and cut me open with a big cross on my stomach. There was an incision on the inside and one on the outside. The outside one goes all the way from my pubic bone to my belly button. Forget ever wearing a bikini again.

Dad flew up from Palm Beach that day. I spent seven days in the hospital before the doctors felt I was well enough to go home. Then when I was okay to go home, there was a huge blizzard, and I was snowed in. Wayne and my father were snowed in together. Wayne kept calling me, saying things like, "Your father wants me to iron the tablecloth!" I just laughed.

In the bed next to me with the curtain drawn, a lovely young couple was being told that their little girl had Down's syndrome. It was the saddest thing. The nurses, aware that the mood in the room was very heavy, let me go into the nursery and sit in a rocking chair with Nick. Parents were not usually allowed in there, but they made an exception that time. God had sent me a message that I was to cherish this beautiful, perfect child. When things got tough, I would always think how lucky I was to have had such a perfect child.

This was helpful to remember because the first two years of Nick's life were as hard as anything I had ever been through. I couldn't understand how people could have more than one of these little darlings. Nick never slept more than about an hour. He didn't nap. He rejected my breast milk at five weeks old and never went back after having a bottle of formula. I felt as if someone had stood me on my head, put me in a corner away from everything else, and told me to function normally. I was exhausted all the time. I didn't know it then, but nineteen years later, I found out that the blood I had been given in the hospital was contaminated with Hepatitis C. In hindsight, I realize I had acute Hep C those first couple of years of Nick's life. I am very lucky, because in 1982, they paid bums for their blood. Who knows who donated their Hep C to me? The really extreme luck is that they didn't give me AIDS. In 1982, I would have been dead with AIDS in a few years.

Other than being constantly tired, I was a very happy mother and wife. I loved being Nicky's mom. He was a beautiful child. He had huge brown eyes and beautiful light brown hair. I let his hair grow until he was about two, and people would come up to us and say, "What a pretty little girl!" Luckily, Nick was too young to be aware of this.

Things went well for our little family until the winter of 1984, when we got a phone call from Wayne's brother Burke. A drunk driver had killed his wife, Mary Lynn. That event turned Burke's life upside down—ours, too. It was a dreadful tragedy. She was very young. They were newly married, and quite probably she was pregnant. After the funeral and getting over the shock, Wayne and Burke began to talk about going into the house building and renovation business together. We uprooted our little family—Wayne, me, Nick, our dog Boo, and her son Bubba, and moved back to Palm Beach after the traditional summer on the island.

I bought a house on Aravale Road in the El Cid section of West Palm Beach. West Palm Beach is full of lovely old Spanish-style homes built in the 1920s. The neighborhood is right next to Lake Worth and looks across the water to Palm Beach. The houses in those days were much less expensive than living on the island of Palm Beach, and many of the now-adult Palm Beach kids lived there. It was closer to all the main attractions in Palm Beach than living on the north end of the island.

I loved the house we bought. We painted it light peach and put up turquoise awnings. It was so pretty. It was stucco, two stories high and had a barrel tile roof. It was on a double lot, so we immediately put in a swimming pool that was as big as it could be while far from the power lines. The house had some wonderful old Spanish features, and it had three bedrooms and two bathrooms upstairs. One bedroom had a fantastic outside verandah covered with an awning. Behind the master bedroom was what used to be called a sleeping porch. It had three sides of windows and I used it as my office. The house was L-shaped, and on the other side of it, across from the pool, was a lovely old courtyard with big old trees, with wild orchids in them and hanging moss. There was a fishpond with a fountain and - we kept goldfish there.

Nicky was enrolled in Pat Lane's baby "school" five mornings a week at the Bath and Tennis Club. Pat had four regular kids, and they spent their mornings playing on the beach, on the swing sets, or in the playroom, which was full of fun things to do. Other kids came and went with the holidays, but the four little regulars went every day and loved it. I would drop Nick off at the club and race west of town to the Scowdens' ranch where I kept my horse, Cooch. I tried to ride five days a week. Dad and Bea also kept horses out there. Dad's horses were always named Sam after the big grey thoroughbred out of Man o' War that he had when I was a child. When I was a kid, I had a grey Connemara pony named Lohengrin, and Dad had Sam. They lived at Jane Firestone's farm in Pittsford, NY, and for spring break, we took them three years in a row down to Southern Pines to ride and hunt.

§

In Florida in the 1980s, I rode with Dad at least two or three of the five times I tried to get out there. He rode until he was about eighty-five years old. It was a wonderful time for us together. Bea also had a big, old horse named Tiny Bit Better. He was almost a carthorse. She tried to keep up with Dad, but it was a joke. She pretended to know how to ride but her lack of skill was obvious and the Scowdens told me that when her horse first arrived she came out allot for lessons in their small indoor ring. And it was a big deal when she managed to just stay on board. We never went faster than a trop with Dad or Bea (who was a much more infrequent rider) it was one of those things she would never just tell the truth about. We wouldn't have cared and been much more helpful , to her, I am sure but she insisted that she had always had horses and grew up riding. It wasn't worth worrying about it but Dad would just roll his eyes at me!

It was great to be able to spend so much time in the saddle. The Scowdens' ranch was next to a five-square-mile equestrian preserve and allot of still undeveloped land. Almost all the land around them has been gobbled up by development now, but a small part of the equestrian preserve still remains.

When I was finished riding, I would race back and pick up Nick, and we would have lunch with my friends and Nick's at the B&T. Many days, we'd eat lunch with Dad. In those days, the children of members could use the club and have lunch there every day. I could also use the club for fourteen full days in the high season and anytime during November and May. It was a pretty good deal for me, I didn't have to spend the money to join.

That winter, my friends Mark Howard-Smith and Chip Rand from the islands moved down. Mark had met his future wife, Pam, and we didn't see too much of him. Chip had recently moved down from NYC. He was working for Wayne painting houses. One night, Wayne, Chip, and Johnny Grant, Wayne's youngest brother, went to a Ramones concert while I stayed home. Wayne was badly beaten, first by one of the concertgoers and then a bouncer. I can only imagine what went on. I found out later that Wayne and Chip were doing a lot of cocaine, even at work.

That March, Wayne and I planned a skiing trip. It would be the first time we'd ever left Nicky, and Wayne's mother agreed to stay with him. Wayne and I went skiing in France with an Australian doctor friend we had met on our honeymoon in Aspen. We flew in and out of London spending almost a week there, and then two weeks skiing. On our way back, we stopped in Geneva to go to their annual car show, and I bought my mother-in-law a gold Ebel watch to say thank you.

Nick was almost three years old then. When we walked in the door, he looked at us and froze. He stood there for about ten seconds, a huge grin came over his face, and he ran into my arms. I'd missed him so much, but he adored his grandmother and was very happy with her.

For Nicky's third birthday, Nick had been given little Shetland pony named Candy by some friends. We borrowed a trailer and brought him to the house on Aravale Road for Nick's birthday party. The pony wouldn't walk with a lead line. Candy, darling as he was, was completely untrainable since he was so small no one that could actually ride and train him could get on him to do just that! Wayne saved the day by putting a child on Candy's back, putting Candy's head firmly under his arm, and walking the little pony and child around. Chip Rand was at the party, and I took the last photo I have of him that afternoon.

§

A few weeks later, Chip borrowed Wayne's truck to move from his apartment in West Palm Beach to the Orthweins' garage apartment on Seaspray in Palm Beach. His mother had just had an operation, and I remember talking about that; she seemed to be doing well. I got an uncomfortable feeling helping him unload his stuff from the truck. I often got a sinking feeling around him, and this night I felt it very strongly. Wayne and I went out to dinner, and when we got back, the truck was back.

§

Two days later, the phone rang. It was Junie Howard-Smith Foster. "Weezie, I've just heard. Chip shot himself. They found him dead in a motel in South Carolina."

I had just seen him. He had been moving. How could he be in South Carolina? None of it made sense. It wasn't possible that tall, handsome Chip was dead. The news was devastating, but the story finally unraveled. The day that Chip borrowed the truck, he had asked his girlfriend to marry him, and she had said no. When he arrived at his new apartment with the truckload of stuff, he found out that he couldn't actually move in for a couple of days, so he put his stuff in the garage. In his depressed state, he dropped the truck off at our house, swung by Mark Howard-Smith's and told him he was going to the island. Mark said he thought it was a little early to go up to the river, since it was only the middle of April, but Chip said he was going anyway and said goodbye. He drove his VW Bug as far as Jacksonville, where at 1 AM he called his girlfriend. Evidently, that didn't go very well.

The next thing anyone heard was from a sheriff in a little town in South Carolina, who called his older brother Doug and got his wife, Kim, telling her they'd found a man dead from a shotgun wound, with a note beside him saying to contact his brother. The note went on to say, "I have wanted to do this for two years or more. I can't live with the way I get." It was unreal.

Doug and Jeff flew down to South Carolina to identify the body. Wayne and I flew to Toronto to be with Patty and the rest of the family. Chip's ashes were shipped to Toronto via UPS and didn't arrive in time for the service. Late that night, they turned up, and Doug had to drive to a UPS depot to pick up the package.

Chip left behind two girlfriends: one in NYC, Sarah, who was small and dark-haired, and Beth in Palm Beach, who was six feet tall and blond. Wayne went over and told Beth, when she heard the news, she kicked at her door and fell down the flight of stairs behind it. She came to the service in a white dress with a huge cast on her leg. Sarah—petite, dark hair, and black dress—cried inconsolably through the entire service. It was and is extremely sad.

Chip was buried on his birthday, July 19, on Juniper Island. The burial game me the first inkling that something was really wrong with Wayne. He was "working" in Palm Beach and refused to come up for the service. We had the most irrational argument about it, and during our argument, he kept coughing. He did finally come up, but said he could only stay a couple of days. He said he had a lot of work to do in Palm Beach , so he went racing back down.

Within two weeks of my arrival, back in Florida, we were in Ed McCabe's tough, confrontational therapy group for addicts. Wayne had gone from snorting coke to smoking crack. That was why he didn't want to come to the river and why he had become progressively more irrational. Ed was a marvel and had helped many people. After a year and a half of intense therapy, which I went through as well, Wayne was considered cured. At this point, I realized that I no longer felt anything for Wayne, but for Nick's sake, and because I wanted to support Wayne in his sobriety, we stayed together. All I had ever really wanted was a good life as a family.

§

Wayne, Nicky and I spent five years on Aravale road. After Wayne got his life back, my father started talking seriously with us about going into the bottled spring water business. We started looking for water plants already up and running to buy, but the costs were way out of our price range. We decided we should try to buy a good spring and build our own plant. We looked all over the East Coast—Northern Florida, North Carolina, Virginia, and upstate NY on the Canadian border north of Plattsburg. Adolphus Busch Orthwein, the stepfather of our friend Michael Montgomery, heard what we were up to and told us that in Cherry Valley, NY, near Cooperstown, where the Busch family had their summerhouses, were many natural springs. As it turns out, the ones on Dolph's land weren't suitable, but with a local real estate agent, Wayne found a gushing spring on the south side of the Great Mohawk Valley. Behind this high plateau is the northern side of the Catskill Mountains.

With a half share investment from Dolph, and the other half from my father and me, we bought the twenty acres of land the spring was on. An old railway line ran through the land, and Wayne had the power company run the power lines and a road into the spring which was a mile from the road. This is where he built the plant. We put in an ozone purification system, botteling machinery and holding tanks in a wonderful big building and we moved the family to the area, to the Fly Creek Valley about 7 miles outside of Cooperstown.

§

A little over a year later, the Cherry Valley Spring Water Company opened for business. We bottled water in five-gallon bottles. I helped set up five or six distributors, and then I bowed out, leaving Wayne to run the show.

Meanwhile, I enjoyed life on our farm in Fly Creek. We bought a wonderful new house that had all the charm of an old farmhouse, and in fact, people took it for a renovated farm, but it was entirely new and had all kinds of modern features. We built a small horse barn and kept three horses, three dogs, and two cats. Wayne started keeping chickens. We painted the house and barn yellow with white trim.

Nicky went to the public school in Cooperstown, and then on to the Indian Mountain School , in Lakeville, Connecticut in the fifth grade. Lakeville was a 21/2-hour drive from us. I was able to go to a lot of games or ski races just for the afternoon, and Nick came home as many weekends as they would let him. I missed him so much, but I have to say that the first morning, when the school bus went by and I was still in bed, it really felt good. Nick loved his school, and he was always very independent, so boarding school worked out well for us.

Life in Cooperstown was fun. I loved our house, had my horses, made some good friends, and was very involved with the Lake and Valley Garden Club. Except for the brutally cold winters, it was almost perfect. It was also close enough to Grindstone take my horses to the island with me in the summers—nearly a perfect setup.

But at some point, the wheels started to come off the bus. Wayne was going to work at the water plant, but there was no growth or expansion. I paid no attention, at first, figuring Wayne was a big boy, and he would make the best of it. Meanwhile, however, Wayne had become best friends with a cousin of our investor Dolph Orthwein, Louis Busch Hager, who owned the Busch family estate on Otsego Lake, called Farmlands. Lou built a fantastic house in the woods and started a hunting and fishing club for his six or eight best friends, called the Fin and Feather Club. This took up more and more of Wayne's time.

One night we had Lou and his wife Tracy for dinner and Lou brought Wayne a couple of Bantam fighting chickens—which was the beginning of the end. Who could imagine that chickens could be the death nail in a marriage but the chicken thing got out of control! Wayne started raising fighting chickens by the hundreds. He had incubators set up in the master bedroom. Baby birds start chirping about twenty-four hours before they're out of the shells, Obviously sleeping though this was impossible so I kicked them out—at which point Wayne set them up in the master bathroom saying if the door was shut it would be fine. He also made some pens for all these chicks in the basement because, he said, it was too cold for them in the barn. The chicks growing rather quickly started crowing at four AM, even when very small, so I was not getting any sleep. One day my friend Debby and her two year old daughter Pam came over to visit. We went down to the barn to see the horses (I used to take this little girl in my lap when I was on board in my ring). When we got down there this attack chicken came after us. Debby ran out of the barn and up to the house screaming. I picked up Pam and swung around to jump into the tack room with her in my arms and hit her head on the door frame while trying to kick away this attacking chicken. Now we shut in the tack room, poor little Pam screaming from fright and being whacked in the head. Debbie went up to the house and called Wayne who had to come home from the water plant and catch the attack rooster and let us out ! This was long before there were cell phones. If Debby hadn't headed for the house we would probably still be standing in that tack room afraid to come out!

Aside from the chickens, everywhere driving me nuts I started to realize that Wayne was paying no attention to the water company. Our accountants started calling and telling me that he wasn't paying taxes and was neglecting things. He became obsessed with hunting, hanging out with Lou, and his chickens. Not surprisingly, I guess, he started going to cock fights himself, in places like Buffalo, which are against the law.

Wayne would not listen to reason. I kept telling him he had to stop before he was arrested, and to get back to work at the water plant. By this time, Lou's grandmother had died, and he inherited what was rumored to be $400 million. He wanted Wayne to go to Africa on safari with him, but I kept telling Wayne, "You don't have $400 million! You have to go to work! You need to take care of the company that my father, Dolph, and I handed you on a silver platter. You have to get rid of the chickens!"

But Wayne wouldn't listen. He gave me some dreadful, irrational arguments on why what he was doing was great and continued with all of it. By this time, I was president of the Lake and Valley Garden Club and had a well-established life in Cooperstown, but my life with Wayne was hell. I wasn't getting any sleep. He didn't care about anything that mattered. He had a few years before stopped doing any family things with Nick and I. He never went to his school games or plays. And he said he never wanted to ski again so to go without him.

I put my foot down. "Either get rid of the chickens, or the marriage is over!" He refused to get rid of the chickens. At first he moved out of the house and into the water plant. When I went to the island, he begged to go back to the house and stay there "just for the summer." I let him, but then I couldn't get him out. I got in touch with a divorce lawyer in Rochester, who told me that since the house was paid for with my money, I could leave without losing ownership of it. So in the fall of 1994, I resigned as the Garden Club president, packed up my Volvo station wagon with my two pit bulls, Boo and Pumpkin, and rented a house in West Palm Beach for the winter. It was gut wrenching and I remember crying while driving for most of the trip down to Florida.

I put the house in Fly Creek on the market, but Wayne had so many chickens and, soon enough, girlfriends with babies that my realtor said some days she couldn't even get her clients into the place because the chickens attacked as soon as they got out of the car.

I divorced Wayne, giving him the water company and keeping the house. I should have done it the other way around, but I was so fed up with all that had gone on that I just wanted out. In the divorce, Wayne was supposed to pay me $1000 a month rent to stay in the house. He never did. It took 2 ½ years to sell the farm and in the end, I took a $100k loss, even though other friends at the time with similar properties doubled their money. My beautiful farm had become a nightmare. Wayne had hundreds of huge fighting cocks stashed in a field away from the road, each one staked out on a chain. It was the worst thing I have ever seen. I was thrilled to finally get rid of place, even at a loss—and out of the marriage.

Ultimately, Wayne let the business go for because he owed $28k in taxes. He owned the twenty acres of land free and clear, and had a viable business going, but he never even tried to raise the money to pay the taxes. The accountants were in disbelief. He sold the business to a man in Cherry Valley who paid Dolph Orthwein back all of his investment. Dad and I never saw a pennyo of the money we had put in. My father was sick about it, but told me at the time that you can't get blood out of a stone, and that I was better off out of the mess.

Nicky was a great support throughout that time. Even at twelve years old, he knew his father was not much of a husband or father. Wayne's idea of fatherhood was picking Nick up by the throat and throwing him up against the wall. The last summer Wayne was with us at the island, Wayne in a fit of rage, smacked Nick across the face, knocking him off his feet.

Nick knew that the best thing for both of us was to get as far away from Wayne as possible. As it turned out, he was much happier seeing his father alone, when he didn't have to hear us screaming at each other. Nick and I have always been able to talk about everything, and we supported and talked to each other through this upheaval. I was happy that he not only understood but supported me as he would do many times over the years.

When it was all over, I rented a darling little three-bedroom pink house right on Lake Worth in West Palm Beach. Nick came down for all his school holidays, and I had my dogs, and sent my horse, Bob, back down to the Scowdens. I had lunch almost every day with my father and sometimes Bea. Bea liked that I was around because it let her go have lunch with her friends and not feel like she was stuck with Dad all the time. This was a wonderful time for Dad and me. I really enjoyed being able to see so much of him.

§

In the spring, I took a trip to Santa Fe, NM, to visit Juliana Seeligson, a good friend from Miss Porter's School. While there, I met Ed Wilson, who had an excellent idea for a tire lock. We came up with the name Pit Bull Tire Lock Corp. The Pit Bull, named after my dog Pumpkin, is a wheel immobilizer for law enforcement and an anti-theft device. Much lighter and easier to use then the old-fashioned Denver Boot, it became used around the world, from the Ministry of the

Interior in Qatar to 250 colleges and universities. It is also a brilliant anti-theft device for a car or a trailer. Most boat thefts happen when the boat is on a trailer. Our biggest anti-theft client was Home Depot Rental Stores, which used them in all their stores in the USA and Canada to secure their rental equipment.

Nick asked if he could come and live with me for the seventh grade before he went off to boarding school again. He had already been readmitted to the Palm Beach Day School, but we talked and decided that Santa Fe would be a good place for both of us. We flew out there in June, and he was admitted to Desert Academy, brand new day school, for the following fall. We were on the move again.

We pulled up stakes and moved into a fantastic house on Cloudstone Drive above the Old Santa Fe Trail. The views were fabulous, and I was able to install the offices for Pit Bull in the house. The Ed and I began working to get the business off the ground. He found a fabricator, Van Baehr, who figured out how to cast the steel rebar in the middle of sand filled aluminum lock to resist cutting tools. It was an exciting time. I ran the business end and organized marketing and sales. Sales were incredible.

I was lucky to have two great friends come on board and help with sales. Katy Keiffer, in NYC, had also gone to Miss Porter's with me, and Charlie Shields, a childhood friend from the Thousand Islands, became our Canadian sales rep. We had a rep in the UK, Nick Andrews, and a few others who came and went. With this little gang we sold quite a few tire locks.

The best part for all of us, I think, aside from making money, were the trade shows we had to attend. I went to many of them with Katy. She and I would share a room and many laughs. We went to Amsterdam, Manchester, Birmingham, London, Toronto, Seattle, Reno, Las Vegas, San Diego, New Orleans, Orlando, NYC, Atlantic City, Boston, and more, making friends with vendors we'd see from one trade show to another.

At one show in Reno, Katy and I were at a booth by ourselves. A vendor we'd recently seen in New Orleans was there. Just as we were unpacking, he came up and told me he had heard I was newly single and wondered why I hadn't let him know. I thought it was a joke and laughed it off. Later, he asked if I would like to have dinner with him at a fancy Reno restaurant. Sensing something was up, I replied, "Katy and I would love to have dinner with you!"

He took us to a strange place filled with fake Greek around to "us." Of course, there was no "us," and Katy, thank god for her, kept helping me steer the conversation elsewhere.

After dinner, we went into the slot machine area next to the restaurant. (Every place in Nevada has slot machines!) While Katy was filler her slots, our "friend" kept pushing up against me until I told Katy we had to leave. The man went back with us to our hotel, and he turned to me and said, "Do you want to go outside and take a walk?"

I replied, "What? You're married, aren't you?"

He said, "Yes, but that shouldn't matter!"

I said, "Forget it. I'm going up to my room. Thank you for dinner and good night."

Katy and I got back to our room and howled with laughter, but we were also a little sad that a man we had liked as a friend was now on the no-go list. We went to bed giggling over the twirling Greek statues.

§

The next morning, we were woken from a sound sleep by the house phone. I had to get out of bed to answer it because it was on the desk. It was our friend from the night before. He was calling to tell me he "wanted to be the first to wish the most beautiful girl in the world good morning!"

Oh, my! My stomach was in a knot. Katy was just stirring in her bed and asking who it was. I said something totally daft into the phone, like "Thank you," and he asked if I would come down and have breakfast with him before he left. I declined and got off the phone, Katy and I shrieking, as girls do.

About fifteen later, there was a knock on the door. Katy and I looked wide-eyed at each other, and I whispered, "I am in the shower. Get rid of him!"

I went into the bathroom, locked the door, and actually got into the shower, too scared to think of doing anything else. Katy somehow got rid of him. We thought, Okay, that's it. He's gone. We took forty- five minutes longer getting out of the room, and as we walked to the elevator banks, there he was. I never needed my friend more than at that moment.

He got in the elevator with us. Katy was brilliant and started right in, saying, "Oh, K, how interesting running into you again here!" I was gobsmacked. Unable to say a word. As we got out of the elevator, he took me aside and said, "I have to have you, you beautiful woman."

I reminded him again that he was married. I scurried along to catch up with Katy and just kept walking. He then said he had to leave to catch his plane and that he would be in touch.

Katy and I to this day squeal with horror and get a good belly laugh from this memory. He rang me a few times after that and tried to keep in touch via e-mail, but I was not interested, and I guess he finally got the message. Occasionally, I still get an e-mail from him, but now it is usually about finding Jesus. I guess he was able to help him where I wouldn't !

Chapter 4

Sea Changes:
Palm Beach, I

After seven years of really enjoying his life there, Dad sold the salmon camp in New Brunswick. Bea had refused to go up there anymore as once again she demanded they move to Newport in the summer. But Dad in those days would have not of that and instead bought a three hundred-acre horse farm in the mountains above Blacksburg, VA. The house, called Thundercroft, was spectacular: it sat on top of a mountain, with a mile-long driveway through walnut and dogwood trees up to a modern house. It had a swimming pool, tennis court, and stables. It suited Dad very well, because he was horseback riding again with me in Palm Beach in the wintertime, just one of the many sports he enjoyed.

The scene always reminded me of the TV show Green Acres. Dad would be in his old work pants and torn straw hat out on his tractor, and Bea would be in her mink, holding their small yapping dogs in front of the Rolls Royce. (She was not allowed to drive the Rolls. Only Dad or I ever drove that car.) Dad even looked a little like Eddie Albert, and Bea dressed and sounded like Eva Gabor with black hair. The only thing missing was Mr. Ziffle the pig.

Bea actually made the best of this place. It wasn't Newport, but they could be on the top of the social pile, giving tennis luncheons and the like. Virginia Polytechnic Institute was in Blacksburg, and the president was, as he should be, an engineer like Dad. He and Dad forged a firm friendship. Dad loved the farm, planting thousands of fruit trees and putting in a vegetable garden (which he had always done in Rochester, Grindstone Island and at the Salmon camp. He even tried in Florida but hated how hard it was to grow even lettuce in the head down there.). He had a small stable for his horses and a kennel for his hunting dogs. In the surrounding countryside, he was able to hunt grouse, woodcock, and deer.

Dad had offered me the house on Grindstone Island back when Bea refused to go there anymore. I had been relieved because I was afraid Bea would make him sell it. Dad said that he knew if he gave it to me, he would always be able to come back. I was twenty-four when Grindstone Island became mine. He told me many times that he was very happy that he was able to do that. He told Dale Bandel, our trust officer, many time that he wanted to make sure I never had to sell the place because he knew how much it meant to me—and to him.

Unfortunately, Dad was only allowed back to Grindstone Island one time after Bea forced him to go elsewhere in the summer. Years ago when Nick was quite small, he and Bea stayed two or three days. He didn't want to leave, but Bea insisted they had to get back. Dad pruned his apple trees, took walks with me in the woods looking for grouse, and visited many of his life-long friends. It was very emotional for him to be there, and he told me that he wanted to be cremated and have his ashes buried out back with our dog Boo. I told him that was where I was going, too, so we would be together.

I asked him then, "What will happen to Bea?"

He said, "She can go down to Miami in a drawer, like her mother!"

We had two more conversations about his wish to be buried on Grindstone Island over the course of the next twenty years. Both of these conversations were in the living room in Palm Beach. On each occasion, he reminded me of what he wanted. I do not know why his lawyer never told him he needed to specify it in his will. He had no trouble changing his will many times for other matters. Why wouldn't he suggest this? It was a normal thing for most people to include in such documents. Dad never did. He even told Dale Bandel once that he didn't want anything fancier than a pine box.

The last thing on earth my father would have wanted was to be put in a mausoleum in a Catholic cemetery that cost almost $100,000. In the first place, he was not Catholic. I'm not sure he even believed in God. This man lost both his parents by the time he was 12. I lost my mother at 15. I understand totally how faith killing that alone can be. He certainly never practiced any faith. The hideous brass casket Bea put him in would have made him sick. I assume he spends his time now spinning in it.

When Nick was two years old, Dad and Bea had a butler named Jorge Silva, who was from Chile. When Dad and Bea were going to go to the salmon camp in Canada, they could not take Jorge because he wasn't legally in this country and wouldn't be able to get back in at the end of the summer. Dad called and asked, since Grindstone Island was in the US, if Jorge could work for us for the summer. He said he would pay him. I did not turn the offer down.

Jorge was twenty-one, gay, and tons of fun. We all got along really well that summer. Nick had an au pair named Laura and the place was a barrel of monkeys with those two in the house.

Jorge was the first of Bea's "servants", as she called them, to confide in me about what it was like to work for this woman. The stories he told me were unbelievable. There were weird, perverted sex ones about her and her dogs that I cannot repeat. But what really horrified me about her character was what she loved most to do was to take the poor maids into her closets and show them all of her dresses and shoes and tell them how much each cost. What an evil cruel thing to do !

She yelled at the help all the time and never treated them with respect. Much of this we had seen over the years. My father, on the other hand, was very kind to the people working for them, but they all spoke mostly Spanish, so only Bea could actually talk to them. It was painful to be around when she was screaming at one poor woman after another. No one left her employ liking her and she was never able to keep people working for her for very long.

Jorge, on the other hand, spoke perfect English. He was from Chile, and his mother was a doctor, but he was gay, and his family could never accept that. He came to the USA, first working for Dad and Bea as a butler, marrying a friend of one of the maid's to get a green card, and finally moving to Silver Spring, Maryland, to work for a family there.

Jorge told us about Bea's new car. When Dad married Bea, she had an old, green Pontiac of some sort, a real bomb. He bought her a gorgeous 500 S Mercedes. It was baby blue with a white leather interior. It never left Palm Beach. When the car was eight or nine years old, she decided she should have a new one, even though this stunning Mercedes had just 8,000 miles on it. Dad said no, that it was a stupid idea. The car was beautiful and collectible, and he thought they should own it forever. Bea said her friends all had new cars, and she would not drive an old car, but Dad continued to say no.

Bea went out, rented a Cadillac, and parked the Mercedes in the garage. She stopped talking to my father, having meals prepared for him (they had a cook), or going to the club for lunch with him. This went on for two weeks, until Dad finally broke down and took her to buy a new car.

This is where Dad picked up the story when I asked him about Bea's new car. At the time, the Mercedes dealer on Okeechobee Blvd. was also a Volvo dealership. When they arrived at the dealership, Bea saw a new silver 740 Volvo. She went nuts for the car, saying, "Oh, Yorge, I love dis Merkceddes."

Dad said, "This one, Bea? This one right here?"

"Oh, yes, dis Merkceddes!"

Dad said, "Bea, it's yours!"

Of course, it was half the cost of the new Mercedes he was prepared to buy.

Dad ushered her out of there as soon as he gave a deposit for the car. He saved himself a small fortune and was thrilled. He hated to sell the Mercedes because he thought it was a stupid thing to do, but if he could replace it with a car cheaper than a new Mercedes, and get Bea off his back, he was happy. For years Dad, Wayne, and I called it the Volvo Mercedes.

Dad always said Bea spent money like a drunken sailor. If you gave her a million dollars, she would spend it. He never trusted her with money, and certainly not with his money. He kept his bank accounts in his name—both his investment account and his checking account. Bea could pay the bills, organize them, and write the checks, but Dad had to sign the checks. Dale Bandel was instructed never to discuss anything about Dad's account with Bea. Dad did of course give Bea a healthy allowance to live on.

§

For six years in the 1990s, Bea's younger brother Fernando lived in two of the maids' rooms over the garage. He lived there rent-free and had the run of the house, as if it were his own. He had cupboards marked with his name on them so that no one would eat his food, yet he sat at the table with Dad and Bea every morning and night eating their food (lunch was almost always at one of their clubs). He did some of the yard work, so I thought, well, if he is doing that, then I guess he's earning his keep, but when I said this in front of Dad one day when Fernando was complaining, Dad said, "I pay him to do the lawn work and he lives here for free."

Fernando drove Dad crazy with his arrogance. Dad hated him. I asked Dad why he didn't just throw him out of the house. Dad replied, "I can't. If I do, she will go, too, and she will take half my money. I can't go through the humiliation of a divorce or annulment again." (He was, of course, referring to the horribly embarrassing two-month marriage to Claire Cooney.)

This was a hard time for my father. He hated putting up with Fernando and the constant threat of Bea leaving him alone when he was well into his 80s.

When Nicky was about ten or twelve years old, Fernando played a game of Monopoly with him. Fernando cheated. Nick had never played with someone who cheated before. I felt this spoke volumes about Fernando's character. He even tried taking funny money away from Nick. Eventually, Fernando did move to a condo in Boca Raton and found a job working at Office Depot. Miriam, Dad's housekeeper, and guardian angel, the last eight years of his life, told Nick and me that one time, Dad caught Fernando, an obvious closet gay, taking a guy up to his room. Miriam said that while Dad was alive, Fernando had the key to Bea's safe deposit box, which was filled with her massive jewels. She owned nothing when she married my father. I think her mother left her some pearls and pearl earrings, and Dad gave her a huge Colombian emerald with ninety-six rectangular diamonds around it. The entire ring is half the size of a golf ball. Dad gave her other emeralds in the first years together, but as she did with many things, Bea hoarded jewels.

§

We went to visit Dad and Bea at Thundercroft, the farm in Blacksburg, VA. many times. Bea had two Westies, a breed she took to after having the little Westie I got when I was fourteen. The dogs were called Chico and Minnie.

The house was very modern. There were two-story windows looking to the southwest with a view over the pool and tennis court with bigger mountains in the distance. There was a stand of beautiful white birch trees next to the pool. On the half-mile drive up to the house, the woods were all walnut trees and dogwood. The drive wound up the hill though the trees. The walnut trees were valuable, and every winter, a few would be cut down and stolen. Around the top forty acres, Dad installed an eight-foot electric fence to keep the deer out.

The first year he owned the place, he planted a hundred fruit trees, and the deer destroyed them all. So up went this fence, which gave you the feeling of entering a low-security prison. You couldn't see it from the house which was a good thing. The fence must have cost a pretty penny, but Dad, showing his Scotch meanness, did not install an electric gate, which seemed the obvious thing, considering the whole thing was electric to begin with, but he had a big gate that you had to open by hand. Because of all the electricity, he had a rope to close it so one would not be shocked to death while coming and going. I always thought it was funny because it could have been a security fence as well as a deer fence, but Dad didn't care about security; he only wanted to keep "the damn deer" out.

One morning, while we were making breakfast, looking out at that lovely view, Bea started telling us she was happy that Minnie was still alive.

"What do you mean, Bea?" I asked.

"Well, Meeennniee keeps trying to co-mit sue-ee-cide."

"What? How?"

"Meeenniee keeps eating cheeepmuncks whole! And the cheeepmunks start eating her from the inside, and I have to take her to the vet to get them out."

My Jaw dropped right down to the floor !

§

After Minnie and Chico died, Bea got two miniature, longhaired dachshunds. Dad hated the dogs. He felt a dog should have a purpose, and he couldn't fathom what they were good for.

These yappy little dogs were not nice to have around. Their names were Benji and Joy. (Joy was named for giving Bea that feeling.) They yapped, as so many tiny dogs seem to do, but the worst part was if you petted Benji, he would pee. As time went on, if you even talked to him, he would pee. When Bea came upon Wayne petting Benji, she was" overjoyed".

She said, "Oh, Vayne, Benji is so happy that you are showing him af-fec-tion. He needs it so much. When he was born his mother rejected him because he was born backwards. So he was reject. He loves you, Vayne, for petting him."

After Tianamen Square, many of the dissidents came to the USA and were placed in US universities. There was a group attending Virginia Tech, in Blacksburg. One came with his wife, who ended up working for Dad and Bea. Her name was Susie. That was not her real name, but that was the name Bea gave her because she couldn't figure out how to say her real name.

"Susie" came to Palm Beach for the winter to work for them. We went to a lobster dinner at the Bath and Tennis Club one night with Dad, Bea, and my friends Steve and Mercedes Gotwald. During dinner somehow, the subject of Chinese people eating dogs came up. We weren't talking about Susie, though. Bea was adamant that we didn't know what we were talking about and that the Chinese did not eat dogs. My father just rolled his eyes and shook his head, and we all gave up. Bea always thought that if she didn't know about it, it must be wrong.

The next day, we were all in the kitchen, and Wayne could not resist.

"Susie, have you ever eaten dog?" he asked.

"Oh, yes, Mr. Wayne. It is very good, but I like monkey better." Bea went white as a sheet and in a panic picked up Benji and Joy and started screaming at the top of her lungs, "Do not eat my doucks! Do not eat my doucks."

Susie gave her a look and said, "Mrs. Ford, I would not eat your dogs. They are too small. In China, we would want to eat a larger dog."

Wayne, Nicky, and I were laughing so hard we thought we would explode. Bea left the kitchen with her dogs, slamming doors as she went.

§

My dear friend in London Robert Buxton loved to tell the story that the first time Bea came to London, newly married to my father, the Buxtons had them and a few other English couples for dinner. Bea told everyone she loved to shoot with my father because she enjoyed the great outdoors so much. (Of course, this was untrue, but she did traipse around with Dad the first few years when they were married, playing the part.) She told the group that they went to Texas to go "doogk" shooting.

The English, who love to shoot, but also adore their dogs, were to say the least horrified . After Dad and Bea left to go back to the Cannought Hotel, the reaction as the door shut behind them was that that they knew Americans loved to their guns, and hunted and shot just about anything, but they were disgusted that Americans shot dogs for sport. Bea, of course, was trying to say "ducks," but her accent was so thick not one person in the room understood her.

§

Dad had a mini-stroke at age eighty, when Nick was seven, and his doctors in Florida and Virginia told him he needed a double heart bypass. My uncle Mort had had heart surgery a few years before, and he never really recovered from it. Dad decided that he had lived a good long life, and if he were going to die, he would rather do it on his own, without major surgery. He decided not to have the bypass.

He then drastically changed his diet, eating no salt, no sugar, no butter, no fat, no meat, and so on. He only ate salmon, wild rice, watercress (instead of lettuce, because you can't put pesticides on watercress). He had never been much of a drinker, but he gave up what little he drank at this point. This vigilance kept him going. He was able to outsmart death for a long time. His will to live was very strong.

§

For the last ten years of his life, Bea had Dad taking melatonin. I was never sure why he was "hooked" on this. I never knew my father to have trouble sleeping. He was always able to take a nap; even when he had his factory, he had a big leather sofa in his office so that he could get forty winks after lunch. Now, it was a little scary. He slept all the time. He didn't get up until eleven AM, and then he had breakfast and slept for another hour, then went to the B&T for lunch, then home to sleep in his chair in the afternoon. As time went on it seemed to get worse and worse. I begged him to stop taking so much melatonin. It was everywhere—by his desk, in his bathroom, next to his bed, in the kitchen. Even after he was unable to drive or move around much in the house, the melatonin was still everywhere. I asked Bea why she was buying him all this melatonin and she told me she didn't buy it. Dad bought it himself. She then went off in a huff. It was impossible.

§

Sometime in the mid-1990s, there was a blowup with Bea and Chase Private Bank. Dad's account was there with Dale Bandel and Brad Greer. Dad's checking account was always overdrawn, and he couldn't figure out why. He would balance the checkbook, and the account never seemed overdrawn when he checked. He asked Dale to check what was going on. Dale said that from what she could see, the money was all going out as cash on a cash/debit card. Dad told Dale to put a $100 limit on the card. I am not sure how Bea ended up with a card on in the first place, because it was not in Dad's nature to give her access to any of his money, but she was regularly making large withdrawals with it. Besides she had an account of her own to use as spending money.

After Dad had talked to Dale and figured it out, and the $100 limit was put on all ATM withdrawals. Bea went into Chase and demanded to know what was wrong with her card. One of the tellers told her that there was nothing wrong with the card, but that there was a $100 limit on it. Bea threw a fit in the lobby of the bank screaming " I am Mrs. Yorge Forth, and you cannot do this to me!"

She caused a big scene and announced that she was removing all "her" money and putting it in a separate bank. Dale told me the people in the bank were shocked by her behavior. She did take her little account out of Chase. Dad, of course, had given all the money in that account to her over the years.

She came to see that Dale was an obstacle to her getting at Dad's money. Bea knew that Dad trusted Dale completely and that Dale and I were friends. On a trip to Palm Beach a few years after this, Dale invited Nick and me to have lunch with her. We told Bea we were going to lunch with Dale, and she went crazy. I had always been good friends with Dale, and Bea had never reacted like this before. She came unglued. I heard Bea call Dale before lunch and tell her that she was not to discuss my father's account with me or tell me anything. It was actually none of Bea's business what Dale and I discussed as I had always had my own account with her from the money my mother left me.

§

By the end of the 1990s, Dad was beginning to show signs of senility—not too surprising, since he'd turn ninety-three in 2000, but nonetheless upsetting. When Dad was ninety years old, seven years before he died, Nick and I spent Christmas in Palm Beach. Dad acted strangely. One day, around noon, just before we were to go to lunch, he was pacing the house. I asked him what was wrong. He said he was waiting for Bea to come back so that we could go to lunch at the club. I suggested that we just go and have her meet us there, leaving her a note.

Dad said, "No, no, she will be back—the stores close at two."

This was so odd and distressing that I called Dr. Warren, who told me it was senility and to be expected at his age. Sometimes his senility was almost amusing. At Christmas in 1999, age 92 1/2 Dad told Nick that he had played baseball for the Baltimore Orioles. This was a good one that we all got a kick out of not least because he was a Yankee's fan his entire life !

§

Around this time, Bea seemed to be making moves to increase her hold on my father—and his money. In May 2000, Katy Keiffer and I came to Florida for a trade show in Ft. Lauderdale. Because Katy was with me, Bea recommended that we stay elsewhere, even though the house had plenty of room for both of us, so we went to a friends house in the north end. One day after lunch, Bea asked me to Dad to his lawyer Jamie Pressley's office in West Palm Beach, and then to the rehab centre in Palm Beach where Dad went once a week to work out in the pool. Dad was pretty feeble by then. I remember standing right behind him on the escalator on the way up, with my arms spread across from one handle to the other because I was afraid he might topple backward. I had to park out in front in a no-parking zone because Dad couldn't walk very far. Dad went into the conference room with Jamie while I sat in the waiting area. He emerged with papers in his hand. I had a very uncomfortable feeling, and I could tell Dad was uncomfortable with me.

I drove him, as instructed, afterward, to the rehab center and was supposed to come back in forty minutes to pick him up. He left the papers in the passenger seat of my rental car. They were just sitting there, and I looked. Included was a copy of a letter from Jamie to my father saying, "This agreement with Bea puts this matter we have just succeeded in ending behind you. I know you don't want to reopen it again, but if you want to ever take the house and put it back in the trust you will have to have Bea's permission to do that." The change to the trust was enclosed.

I was in shock. Bea had managed to get the PB house out of the trust. Under the old arrangement, Bea would have had use of it until she died, when it would revert to me, and then Nick, even though she had no children in the first place, and the house had always been owned only in my father name. I didn't know where else to go, so I took the papers to Dale Bandel.

She took one look at them and said, "This looks bad."

I had to go pick up Dad. I went in to get him and when he got in the car, I said, "Here are your papers, Dad."

He took them and we drove back home, he left them again, and I saw them when I got back into the car, after helping him up the front stairs to the door. I was coming back to go to dinner with Dad and Bea, so I decided to take the papers back to my friends house and copy them on the fax machine, and then give them to Dad when I saw him for dinner. When I arrived to pick up Dad and Bea, I had the papers in my hand. I handed them to Dad and said, "You forgot these in my car."

Bea went white as a sheet. Needless to say, we did not have a convivial dinner. Dad was crabby, Bea bitched at the waitress the entire time, and I just felt sick.

I cried myself to sleep that night. It felt like no matter how good a daughter I was, I could never win. Bea had made my relationship with my father into a battle for his money, which had never been part of our lives. She worked to maneuver me out of any position. I was much too afraid to speak about such things with my dad. I mean, one just didn't . I only started fighting for myself when I got desperate. But it didn't help anything in the long run. In fact it probably only made Bea circle her wagons even tighter and the older and more feeble Dad became the stronger she was.

§

In May 2001, three and a half years before Dad died, I was diagnosed with Hepatitis C, which I got when Nick was born in 1982. By the time I found out, I had had it for nineteen years and the damage to my liver was extensive. Measured on a scale of 0 to 4, mine was stage 3. My doctor said I needed to go on a course of interferon and ribavirin. The interferon was prescribed as a shot I would give myself in my stomach once a week, and the ribavirin was eight pills each day. I didn't have health insurance, and because the hepatitis was "a pre-existing condition," a new policy would not cover it. The timing of all this could not have been worse. I had just run out of the money my mother left me at her death.

I had a friend who also had Hep C, and he saw a specialist in Boston—Dr. Fredrick Gordon. I decided to get a second opinion, as the treatment was severe. I told Dad that I wanted to see Dr. Gordon, and Dad said he wanted to come with me. I made reservations at a hotel across the street from Dr. Gordon's office.

Dad and Bea were in Newport for the summer. I spent one day in Newport with Dad and Bea. When I arrived, I was shocked at how much Dad had deteriorated since my visit to Palm Beach the previous Christmas. He had a huge black-and-blue mark on the side of his face. He told me he had fallen down the stairs. The house they bought just that year in Newport was an old garage converted into a house. It had obviously belonged to the huge Newport mansion across the street at one time. The top floor was not unlike the one over the garage in Palm Beach; it had four small bedrooms and one bathroom that we all had to use. The downstairs, obviously once the garage, was open, except for a small study with a bathroom off it. Dad should have been using that for his bedroom, as he was not at all steady on his feet, but Bea had him going up very narrow, winding stairs. I now wonder if he might have been hurt in some other way. He had no bruises on his body, only on his face. Falling down the stairs should have caused some bruises to his body, I thought.

§

I arrived in Newport on a Saturday at the end of July. We went to the NY Yacht Club for dinner that night and Bailey's Beach Club for lunch on Sunday. Before lunch, I went into the study where Dad was watching the Sunday morning political talk shows.

Bea joined us and turned down the volume on the TV. She turned to me with a big smile on her face and said, "Weezie, what was that name of that nice boyfriend you had? You know, the conservative one? The really nice conservative one? When we lived at Lost Tree?"

I said, "You mean Tom Brush from Boston?"

She said, "Oh, yes, that's the one! I remember you had a very big fight with him."

I said " I did? I don't remember ever fighting with him."

She said, "Oh, yes, you did. You told him you were a Charles Manson follower, and he told you how wrong you were."

I said, "What the heck are you talking about? That conversation never happened."

Bea exclaimed, "Oh, yes, it did."

"No, it didn't!"

"Oh, yes, it did, dear. I remember it well. You remember it, too, George, don't you?"

Dad turned to Bea sheepishly and said, "Yes, Bea, I do."

I was flabbergasted. (Afterward, I looked up Charles Manson on the internet. I was thirteen years old and going to Sacred Heart in Rochester, NY, when those murders happened in southern California.) I could hardly believe it, but it showed me that she could get Dad to agree to anything she said and make him think terrible things about me that were not only untrue, but also truly insane.

The rest of the day went on normally if that is possible after being told you were a follower of one of the worst mass murders in my memory and I was truly shaken by the conversation. Dale Bandel told me later that she took Dad and Bea to lunch after she moved to Citi Bank, and Bea told her that story, too. Dale said she replied, "I can't believe it. Weezie listens to Rush Limbaugh."

§

That afternoon, Dad and I were to drive up to Boston for my appointment the next morning. At lunch, before we were to leave, Bea told me that she had changed our reservations to another hotel because the one I had booked was too expensive. All I wanted to do was spend money, she said. I told her the doctor's assistant had suggested that hotel. She told me that Dad would ride with her because he could not ride in my car. That's how I learned she intended to come along. It was such a heavy-handed power play that I felt slapped across the face with it. I wasn't plotting anything, I just wanted my Dad with me to find out about my illness, and he had wanted to go with me.

We arrived at the hotel Bea had chosen, and it was a slum. Really bad. We had to move to the hotel I had originally booked because it was so bad. The entire trip had become nightmarishly uncomfortable. Bea kept giving me evil stares, and Dad was acting sheepish and down trodden. We all went to the doctor in the morning. Dr. Gordon called me in, and I asked Dad to come with me. Bea said she had to come, too. Not one to make a scene, I said okay, but with her came the uncomfortable feeling.

Dr. Gordon was great. He spent an hour with us explaining the disease and its progression. He even used a chalkboard. Bea kept asking really stupid questions, but he patiently answered them. "How can Weezie get these drugs for free?" "Can't the government support her?"

Dr. Gordon said if I lived in Boston, he could put me in a trial. Bea said, "Oh, that's what you must do."

I asked how that would work? I live in Santa Fe, I said, and run my business from there. I couldn't move to Boston for a year. Where would I live?

Bea said I could live in their house in Newport. "You must do it," she said, "and then we will not have to pay for the treatment."

My father, finally having had enough of her nonsense said, "Don't worry, Dr. Gordon. Of course, I will pay for Weezie's treatment."

I thought Bea was going to kill him right then and there, and if Dr. Gordon hadn't been in the room, she probably would have. She was seething.

I have no idea why Bea thought the government would take care of me. I was not exactly on welfare. I owned my home in the Thousand Islands and ran a small business. I don't know if she thought we lived in a country with a national health system or what, but then, many things this woman said never made sense.

After this visit, I went back to Santa Fe, and at the end of October, after a trade show I was already committed to do, I started my treatment. Dad had Dale Bandel deposit $9,600 in my account each month for nine or ten months, to cover the costs, but the first couple of months Bea would not let me talk to him on the phone, and Dale and I could not get the payments set up. Dale finally got through to my Dad and told him what needed to be done to get these payments to me and Dad instructed her, while being recorded to take care of it.

After this, Bea wrote Dale a letter, supposedly from my father, printed out from her computer. (Dad never knew how to type; he only knew how to dictate to secretaries.) She then had Dad sign it. It said that from now on, no money was to be transferred to Weezie unless Dale received a letter with Dad's signature on it. Needless to say, Dad was unable to write such a letter at this point. By doing this, Bea stopped Dad from helping me ever again with money unless she first wrote the letter and he signed it, but for now, with Dale's help keeping Dad on track, I was able to get through the treatment.

I started the treatment on my own. Nick was in his first year at the University of Nevada at Reno. My business partner, Ed Wilson, had run off with a German woman and had given up doing anything with the company. I didn't know it was possible to become a drug addict in your forties, but Ed did.

Around this time, Wayne was looking for work, and after some thought I offered him a job as my assistant. He and I were friends now.

He could answer the phones and run the company when I had my "down" days.

Nick said to me, "Wayne is a nice guy, but you can't count on him for anything," and he hit the nail on the head. After promising to come out to Santa Fe when the treatment started, it took him two months to disengage himself from a girlfriend named Summer (whose brother's name was Storm). When he did come, I paid him to work for me, and helped him buy a new Subaru and a laptop. He did a pretty good job of covering the phones when I was unable to. By then, I really needed the help. He owed me a lot of money for child support, but told me that he would pay me when he could. I tried to get him to work for part of his debt, but he said he wouldn't do it if that was the deal. Beggars can't be choosers.

The treatment for Hep C is no fun. Some people take it better than others do, or so they say, but I have never met anyone who actually took it well. The day I started my treatment, I went to the doctor's office around four PM. He showed me how to give myself the interferon injection in my stomach. I had a terrible time doing that. I had to grab a wad of fat on my belly—luckily, this was not a problem—stick the needle in under the skin, and then push. All this was after having to mix two mixtures in two small bottles, testing for bubbles in the syringe, and trying to stop myself from shaking like a leaf. I went through this treatment two separate times, and I never got over shaking and sweating while injecting myself. The interferon burned going in, and for a couple of weeks there was a big red/purple mark at the injection site. This was a good thing in one respect, because it kept me from injecting myself in the same place the following week, which would not be a good thing. My stomach became a mass of red, sore blotches two inches in diameter.

That first time, I gave myself the injection in the doctor's office and then ingested my first round of eight ribavirin pills, the daily dosage. Then I had to drive home, up the hill in Santa Fe to my house, and wait. First, I lay down on the sofa. Nothing happened. I thought it was weird, but maybe I would be one of the lucky ones with no symptoms. At about eight PM, I got into bed and started to read. Then it started. At first, for at least two hours I was freezing. I felt nauseous, but I had to keep getting up to put on more layers of clothing. No matter what I put on, however, I shivered uncontrollably. My teeth were chattering. I looked like the Pillsbury doughboy in my socks, long underwear, fleece, and cashmere sweater under the down duvet. Nothing worked. I was just cold from the inside out. Then, after a good two hours, I started to burn up. Off came all the clothes. I was shaking and sweating up a storm. I am not sure if I got any sleep at all that first night. I was freaked out by what was happening to me, and I kept worrying that I would pass out. I kept the phone right next to me in case I had to dial 911. I was all alone, and that felt very scary. I can still feel the feeling and the severity of the head ache. Even now as I sit here and write this.

§

The next day, I felt like I had been run over by a Mack truck. I was as weak as a kitten and couldn't lift my head off the pillow. I honestly don't remember if I was alone all day or not. It was all a blur. This was my life for the next 9 months. I got smart after this first time, and my doctor had suggested, take a 5 mg Valium with the shot so I could sleep through the worst of it.

Every Sunday night, I took the Valium, gave myself this dreadful shot, and then climbed into bed. The following day was like the night of the living dead. It was almost impossible for me to lift my head from the pillow. I could barely put a sentence together. On one of these days, I talked to my father in Palm Beach, and he was so concerned he called Dale Bandel and told her he was afraid I was dying. I certainly felt like I was.

The day after the shot was better. I was able to get out of bed and have a massage to try to work the toxic chemo out of my muscles, which ached terribly from the drugs. I remember walking from my car to my massage therapist's house, moving so slowly that it was as if I was ninety years old. (I knew I wasn't safe on the road, but I drove anyway.) This state is called the "interferon fog," and I certainly spent a lot of time in it.

I managed to carry on like this for two months before Wayne finally came out to Santa Fe from the east coast. He could handle the phones on my down days, and he would even run to Jamba Juice in Whole Foods to get me a giant Jamba that tasted so good when I was feeling bad.

As the week progressed, I improved somewhat. By Saturday and Sunday, I felt good enough to go out to the stable and ride my horse, Bob. Of course, I was only able to walk out on him; I would have fallen off at a trot. But it made me feel good to get out under those bright blue Santa Fe skies and enjoy the great outdoors, even though I was unable to hike or do any of the other things I love to do outside. I did try to ski in Santa Fe with my friends Kim and Keith Meredith, whom I had met in Vail a few years before. I took all of two runs and that was that, but at least I didn't go an entire winter without skiing.

After nine months of the treatment, I had not cleared the virus, and the doctors took me off the drugs. They said that I was one of the 52% that were non-responders. At some time in the future, I could try again, but this round had not worked. Just what I wanted to hear.

Memories

Mortimer, William F. (my grandfather) John & George Watters with their mother - Rebecca Byrnes Watters circa 1890

Rose Annette Gavin circa 1895 (my grandmother)

William F. and Rose Gavin Watters in their 1906 "American Mercedes" William at the wheel and Rose over his left shoulder with the smaller hat. On the road from Buffalo to Rochester. Circa 1906.

Rose, Mortimer, William and Mary Louise Watters 1921

U.S. 14 ft dinghy team on board the "S. S. Manhattan" traveling with their 4 boats in the hold. The team was sponsored by the Rochester Yacht Club. My father George E. Ford - Captain (kneeling bottom left) With him was Hal Clark, Charles Tarr, Kimball Flint, Norman Cole, Bill Tarr, Sherman Farnham (back row second from right) and Ed Phillsbury (from Minniapolis) Sherman Farnham and Ed Pillsbury came directly from their Yale graduation to catch the boat. They travelled 7,000 miles sailing in regattas at Aalboorg, Denmark, Oslo, Norway, Hamburg Germany, Firth of Clyde and Cowes England Dad won most of the races included the Prince of Wales Cup. April thru mid Aug 1935.

Mary Louise Watters age 21

Venture III

Mary Louise Watters & George Edward Ford on their wedding day 1940. They had an informal church wedding out of respect for the war in Europe.

George Caroll, Secretary of the Lake Placid Club, giving me my first Snowbird's ski medal age 4.

*My parents and I skiing at
Mt. Whitney, Lake Placid
Club, NY. February 1964.*

*My mother and I in Rochester, NY
the day I posed to have my portrait
painted, age 8*

Dad & I, Palm Beach 1979

*Mrs. Louise Ford Grant Bath and
Tennis Club Palm Beach. November
28, 1980.*

Louise, George & Bea Palm Beach 1979

Louise Ann Ford Palm Beach 1979

*Nicholas George Grant
Palm Beach Day School, age 6*

Nicky and me Vail 1999

*Dad then age 90 & me sailing
Venture VII*

*To Louise
Best Wishes,* G Bush
London 2004

London 2008

Nick & Alanna Grant July 2011 Grindstone Island

Nicky & me July 2011

Weezie Grindstone Island July 2011

Peter McDermott and me July 2011

The Children of Juba, Southern Sudan June 2006

Chapter 5

Loss:

Palm Beach, II

In the summer of 2001, a couple of people expressed interest in buying the Pit Bull Lock Company. I was running it on my own, paying staff and Wayne to help me, and was happy at the idea of getting out from underneath it. About a year before this, Ed Wilson, who had started the company with me and had had the original idea for it, walked away from the company to pursue other interests. That left Van Beahr and me running the show on our own. I could not have done it without Van. From start to finish , he was rock solid. He came up with the way to make the whole idea work. He fabricated the finished product in the shop at his home for the first few years until we got a warehouse space to use as a small factory. Through thick and thin, Van was great to work with, and he and I managed very well to keep it up and running. I know he feels the same way, because he told me afterward what a pleasure it had been working with me.

I sold Pit Bull to Patrick Moynihan. He had been an original investor so he had a stake already. That fall, I did the Parkex trade show with Patrick in London, and realized that when I finished training Patrick's office staff to run the company in New Jersey, I would be free to move back to London. Nick was at University, my horse needed retiring and Nicky could keep Pumpkin. It was a door that opened and I was not about to go through it.

While there for the trade show, I found my flat. It was bright and sunny with lovely views, newly redecorated, and perfect for me. It even had a small extra bedroom for Nick. It was on Chelsea Green, right in the center of where my friends all lived and where I had lived before. All those visits, once or twice a year, had been to this neighborhood. I was thrilled with the place. The only hitch was that because I didn't have a current bank account, the realtors wanted six months' rent in advance. I didn't want to use up so much of the money

I was paid for the company on prepaid rent, so I called Dad and asked if he could pay it for me. He told me he would be happy to do it, and we talked about arranging to have Dale do it. As we were almost done with the call, I heard a beep and realized that the entire conversation had been taped. Meaning Bea heard it all.

I actually wound up paying the deposit and six months' rent on my new flat out of my Pit Bull money because Dad had said he would re-reimburse me. As it turned out, he didn't. In fact, he then told me, with Bea screaming, "She's a liar, she's a liar," in the background, that he had never told me he would do so and that I was a liar.

In the midst of all this, in the fall of 2002, I looked up Professor Roger Williams in London, whom my Boston doctor, Dr. Gordon, had recommended. He told me he was the world's top specialist in Hep C treatments and liver transplants. I started seeing him at the Princess Grace Hospital in a private clinic. He felt I should go back on ribavirin to try to keep my viral load in check. I agreed, although it was very expensive. I called my father again to ask for help. He told me he would be happy to help. However, counting on him was impossible because Bea would thwart everything. I know my father never wanted things to be like this between us but Bea was unrelenting in her quest to have it all. Although at the time I really didn't understand how far she would go to do just that!

§

In the winter of 2002-2003, I had a terribly hard time trying to get my father on the phone. I would get the automated answering machine that would come on after one or two rings. Bea was obviously screening and when she heard it was me the phone was never picked up. I finally had my friend Jackie Cowell tell me when Bea was due to play tennis at the Bath &Tennis Club, they played in the same group, and I would call the house then, begging Miriam, the long-suffering housekeeper, to put him on the phone. She did so most of the time, but she was very scared and said one time, "Oh, no. Mrs. Ford say no!"

I had another friend e-mail me when Bea had an appointment outside the house so that I could call and talk to Dad. If Bea was home, forget it. She would not let me through. She would let the answering machine pick up and then not answer when she heard my voice, or she'd tell me Dad was asleep. If he was around, she might answer the phone and say, "Hello? Hello? Hello? Hello?" and then—click—she would hang up. This kept him from knowing I was on the phone. On the other end, I would be saying, "Bea, it's me. PLEASE let me talk to my father!"

My phone calls were not all about money. I loved talking to my father about many things, such as politics, and we had always talked regularly no matter where I lived. But I was having a rough time of it, and if Dad had been my dear old Dad still, I would not have been in this situation. Other than Bea, I was the only person he would confide in. Over the years, I am sure he confided quite a bit more in me then he did in Bea. She had separated him from his old friends. The people they socialized with were not his friends at all, but ones she felt would help her climb the Palm Beach social ladder. It was all about names and money for her.

§

During the winter, things started to get desperate. Though I continued to hold out hope, I realized that Dad was not going to be allowed to help me with health care costs, as I had counted on and he had promised. I wrote multiple emails to Bea saying if Dad were unable to help me financially, I would love to come home and help care for my father, whom I knew could be quit a hand full, especially given that the only help she had was poor Miriam. I meant it. I wanted to be able to spend time with Dad before he died, and this seemed to me the perfect solution. I would come back from London, live in the house, and really help. Bea replied that under no circumstances would I be allowed to live in her house. When I pointed out that Fernando had lived there for six years, she said that had nothing to do with me.

My cousin Rosemary, Uncle Mort's daughter, wrote at least two letters to Bea trying to convince her to help me. Bea's oldest friend from her days in NYC, Dagmar Buxton (the mother of my old boyfriend Simon Ortiz-Patino), lived now in London with her wonderful second husband, Robert, and adores me. Dagmar had written to Bea before and now wrote again, trying make sure Bea understood how serious my condition was so that she could support my father in helping me.

After I knew these letters had arrived, I called Dad. Bea put the call through right through, by passing her rather efficient screening system. Dad was put on the phone quickly, but the letters, or Bea's reaction to the letters, had made him answer in an angry voice. He said, "You have been telling lies about Bea. That cousin of yours has written terrible letters to Bea, full of lies. Dagmar has written a very mean letter full of lies. You have been saying terrible things about Bea."

I was so shaken by this verbal attack. I asked him whether he had read Dagmar's letter, and asked how he knew what was in it since it was in Spanish, and he didn't speak Spanish. That seemed to sort of make sense to him. I told him that the letters were about me, my health, and my health and had nothing to do with Bea.

These calls were awful because they showed how hard Bea was working to get my father to distrust and hate me. I was and am still terribly hurt by this, because Dad and I loved each other very much, and even if he hadn't been the most traditional, stay-at-home father in the world, he and I had gotten through terrible times together. We had always been able to turn to each other, and now Bea had taken my father from me.

I was able, however, to get Dad to pay for Nick's tuition that year because he had always done so. Nick and Dad were very fond of each other. When Nick was a young and active boy, my father hadn't known exactly what to do with him, but now they were able to talk to each other, they both enjoyed this hugely. That Christmas, 2002, Nick came to London to be with me, because Bea had told us we were not welcome in Palm Beach. She told me Miriam was going to be away and that it was not a good time for us to come down, as we would have to do our own brooming. (Brooming ?) "Bye now," she chirped as she hung up. I felt emotionally damaged by Bea, and a year of the chemo didn't help.

We spent a wonderful Christmas in London with Nick's adorable girlfriend Alanna Clark. (Alanna is the great granddaughter of one of Dad's old friends from the river, Bob Cox.) We had Christmas morning with Alec and Anne D'Janeoff in their flat around the corner, and then went up to Walshaw, Lord Savile's shooting estate, to be with my new best friend Margaret Lumley-Savile and her triplet sons, James, Peter, and Robin. It was a perfect holiday. Walshaw, a huge, old, stone hunting lodge on top of the West Yorkshire moors, it is magic in every season. Emily Bronte used the house on the top of the moors as the setting for Wuthering Heights. The house seems to be on top of the world. It has amazing vistas and some of the best hiking in England.

I did go down to Palm Beach by myself in January 2004 and stayed with my wonderful friend Nellie Benoit. Thank goodness for my wonderful friends. This was to be Dad's last year and I was really worried about him.

During this trip, Dad told me that he had fallen down one day on a pile of rugs. Bea had, in some places, stacked as many as three rugs on top of each other. Dad said that he had had to lie on the floor for a long time because Bea could not lift him off the floor. She eventually called Miriam at her home in Lake Worth to come and help lift him. I told Dad that we should get Bea to get rid of some of the rugs and he replied, "Oh, please, don't make a fuss. It is very bad for me if you say anything to her."

I felt sick. Dad was obviously afraid of her. I kept my mouth shut.

On this trip, I saw that as Dad got older and weaker, Bea ever gaining more control. I later learned that Dad's previous doctor had given him a competency test around this time. Miriam had been with Dad and Bea at the doctor's when Dad failed the test, which his later doctor, Dr. Ness, said his records clearly showed.

Bea's real victory occurred just after this doctor's appointment, when she succeeded in having Dad's money moved from Chase Bank to US Trust. Bea must have felt it was now or never with Dad going downhill the way he was. She was still able to get him to comply with her wishes without going too off track. The living trust had previously been his money alone, but after the move, both Dad and Bea were trustees. Bea now was a co-signatory on his checks. This had never been the case before, and it would not have happened if the account had stayed with Dale Bandel who had moved the previous year from Chase to Citi Private Bank, and Dad's account had gone with her.

The move from Chase to Citi had not been easy. Bea didn't want Dad to follow Dale from Chase and did everything she could to stop it from happening, but one day, Dad and Bea went into Chase, which had recently been taken over by JP Morgan, and a black woman was even have a black gardener work for her. If a gardener came with a black helper, she would fire them. After this woman helped them, Bea's unfathomable prejudice was the catalyst for Dad out of that bank. So Dad moved his money to Dale at Citi.

Only problem was that Dad needed to sign the paperwork for his trust to change the trustees from Chase to Citi (ie Dale) . Bea knew that Dale was protecting Dad's money from her, and she devised ways to prevent Dad from going to his lawyer Jamie Pressley's office to sign the paperwork making the move legally binding. Dale told me that although Dad had moved his money to Citi so it would remain with her, he had not signed the codicil in his will to change the institution from Chase to Citi. She and Jamie had been trying to get Dad in to do so, but had been unable to get past Bea's roadblocks. Bea would keep both Dale and Jamie at bay with her efficient yet dreadfully annoying telephone blocking system. Dale was afraid Dad would die and the account would go back to Chase. Now I think that this is what Bea was hoping for. It would get the money away from Dale. Which she must have figured out by then was better for her because Dale would always follow Dad's wishes to the letter.

Dale asked me to call Jamie Pressley. When I did, Jamie said, "Let me make an appointment for tomorrow afternoon. I will give you a note saying that Mr. Ford has an appointment to see me. If Bea gives you a hard time about it, you can show her this letter."

Dad, Bea, and I went to lunch on the Everglades Club golf terrace. I said, "Dad, you have an appointment with Jamie Pressley's this afternoon. I'll run you over there, okay?"

I showed them the letter Jamie had given me.

Bea said, "What? He cannot have an appointment. I have to be asked. I am his wife. You cannot take him unless I am asked first. George, that lawyer is a shyster. All he wants is your money."

Dad said, "Yes, Bea, you're right. He is a shyster! They all want my money. Damn him!"

I went to the parking lot of the club with my cell phone to tell Jamie that I had been unable to get Dad there. I told him about the way Bea had worked Dad, and during this conversation, Jamie said, "I feel very sorry for you."

After I left Palm Beach, Dale and Jamie got Dad to sign that document by finally coming the the house, ensuring, so everyone at the time thought, that Dad's money would stay Dale's capable hands, where it had been for over twenty five years.

§

Later that spring, in one of my rare triumphs in getting Dad on the phone he would be moving his money banks. I asked where on earth he was going to go with it but he couldn't remember the name of the bank it was moving to! Dad told me he was changing banks because Dale was stealing his money. I was astounded. I said, "Dale isn't stealing anything. If your money is disappearing, your wife is taking it."

I freaked about the bank move and called Mike Simon, my Palm Beach attorney, fearing that Bea would move his money to a bank run by one of her Colombian cousins in Miami. Mike called Jamie Pressley's office and was told that the account was going to US Trust. Gary Lickle was then the president of US Trust in Palm Beach and I called him, slightly reassured as I thought I had a friend running the bank. Gary and I had known each other since1980. He and his wife Dragana came to my wedding just two weeks after their son was born. It was their first outing after the birth. I was convinced Gary would listen to me, so I tracked him down in Naples, Florida, where he was staying at the Ritz Carlton. We talked twice. He called me back the second time at three AM, my time.

I told Gary to be sure that the money stayed Dad's money and not put it into Dad and Bea's name. It had always been Dad's money alone, and Bea's name had never been allowed on the account. I begged him to call Dale Bandel to find out how Dad had always handled this account. Gary told me I had nothing to worry about; nothing would change when Dad's account moved to US Trust.

Gary told me to call US Trust and speak to either Liddie or Judy Golumbeiwski. When I spoke to Judy, I told her everything I had told Gary. I was relieved that Gary would look out for my dad. Obviously, Gary didn't give a damn what I had to say. The account became both Dad and Bea's, and Gary told me he could no longer talk to me. Gary had promised that nothing would change at US Trust, but nothing about Dad's account was the same from the minute it arrived there.

With the account now in both their names, Dad could not do anything with his money unless Bea okayed it. No one ever told Dale that the account was leaving. After almost thirty years of putting up with my father, which was not easy, she just got a transfer order. No letter, no phone call—nothing. I was in shock. I got along with the help of some wonderful friends and family, who I thank God for every day.

§

In May 2003, one day after this bank move, Bea moved with Dad to Newport for the summer. When they bought the Newport house the year before, Dad had wanted to put it in his name and mine and said so to Dale's assistant, Lynn Chase. Bea went berserk in front of Lynn screaming " It is my house not Weezie's over my dead body! You put the house in my name!" and forced Dad to put her name on it instead of mine. Mike Simon felt Bea and Dad's speedy exit from Palm Beach was probably meant to get him out of the state so that I couldn't do anything about the outlandish move to US Trust.

§

On June 4, Nick, who was then eighteen, and his girlfriend Alanna went to visit my father in Newport. Nick looked forward to introducing his grandfather to Alanna. We all adored her and Nick knew Dad would, too, but she wasn't given much of a chance.

Nick and Alanna spent one night there. The next morning, Bea went out and they both heard my father banging on his bedroom door to get out. Alanna went to let him out, but the door was locked. A few minutes later, Bea came home, and Alanna said, "Why is Mr. Ford locked in his bedroom?"

Bea told her, "It is for my husband's convenience." Alanna had no idea what that meant. A little later, Dad was sitting in front of the TV in his study. I had recently stopped taking my antiviral drug, ribavirin, because it was so expensive, and Nick took it upon himself to ask Dad personally to help me financially so I could resume the treatment. Dad told Nick that he would go get the checkbook. He shuffled out to the sunroom where Bea was sitting and asked for the checkbook. Bea started unrelentlesly screaming at Dad, and after about ten minutes, the two of them came into Dad's study.

Bea began screaming at Nick, shouting, "Your mother must get the government to take care of her. We cannot pay for you to go to school and your mother's medical costs."

Nick said, "Fine, just pay for Mom."

Bea screamed, "No! Nothing! Your father stole $250,000 from your granddaddy!" Of course, this was untrue, but Dad was well past standing up to her or knowing what was true or untrue. Bea told Nick to leave the house.

It didn't take much to make Nick decide that it was a good idea to leave, so he and Alanna got out. During this scene, my father kept calling his grandson Wayne, further showing his confusion. As he was leaving, Nick said to Bea, "You finally got what you want, Bea. Me and my mother out of Granddaddy's life. I used to hate it when you kissed me and told me how much you loved me, when I knew you hated me. Even as a little kid I knew it."

Bea just stood at the door with her mouth open and locked the door behind him when he left.

After this, Bea kept him away from me, his only daughter, and from Nick, his only grandson. Nick never saw him again. Dad's money had been taken over by people Dad didn't know, and Bea was running the show.

I was not welcome in Newport so I didn't attempt to see my father there that summer. I went to Grindstone Island and then back to London. I went to work for a dress designer as a business consultant the next autumn and just got on with things. Soon, however, I decided to visit my father, as I had never gone as long as a year without seeing him. I booked a trip to visit in January 2004. If I persisted, or if Miriam took pity on me and let me through, I could reach Dad on the phone. I talked to him about my decision to visit, and he was thrilled. He asked me to stay in the house with them this time. Of course, this was what I really wanted to do. I left a message on the answering machine saying when I would be arriving and that I was really looking forward to seeing both Dad and Bea. I was trying to be diplomatic, thinking it was the best way forward. Bea very unlike her normal behavior actually called me back. Afterward, I wrote this summary of the conversation:

Conversation with Bea Ford, Saturday, 10 Jan. 2004, 5:45 AM EST/ 10:45 AM GMT

Bea called to let me know that under no circumstances was I allowed to be alone with my father and that I was not welcome in "her" house. She said that I was allowed to visit him, but only with an appointment and only with her in the room. He was very happy with her, and I only caused disruption.

I told her it was my father's house, and he wanted me to come. Dad was excited about my coming to see him and wanted me to stay in the house. I told her it had nothing to do with causing trouble, but she was trying to keep hold of his money, which was why she had him move banks, and why she was now able to sign checks and would not allow him to give the bank any instructions over the phone, insisting that they be in writing.

I told her that she was treating him as if he were incompetent. Bea said US Trust told her to be the signer on the checking account and that all orders should be taken by letter only. She said she had nothing to do with it. The bank came to her and asked her to do it this way. I reminded her that she had started this letter thing when Dad's account was still with Dale, and Dale did not ask her to do this. She told me that I hated her and had never accepted that she was George's wife, that I just wanted to cause trouble and that she just wanted peace and quiet.

I decided that saying any more about what I knew would only make her go into an even bigger tailspin, so I backed off. I made an "appointment" to meet at the house and go to the B&T for lunch with her and my father on Tuesday after I arrived.

After this conversation, I left two phone messages, the first one asking to use one of their cars as Dad had told me I could. In the second message, I said I had only wanted to come and have a nice visit with my father, and she had made the whole thing into a big scene. There was no reply to either of my phone messages.

This was extremely distressing. I had been at the hairdresser getting my legs waxed when she called. The poor girl who was working on me was brand new, and I was crying and begging Bea on the phone to not be so cruel. I kept saying I loved my father and he loved me and wanted me with him. I was so upset. After I hung up, I realized I needed a place to stay. My friend Nellie told me I was welcome to come to her house. She was horrified that I was only able to be with my Dad for lunch at the B&T during the day.

At lunch, Bea kept ordering Dad vodka and OJ. I was shocked, as Dad hadn't more than a few drinks of alcohol in years, ever since his heart scare, and never at lunch. He was out of it. People would come up to say hello, and he had a blank look on his face. He spilled his food all over himself and the floor. It looked like a two year old had been sitting there when he was done eating. Bea had us eating in the bar because Dad couldn't make it into the dining room. Even so, when we were coming in, I had to run and get a chair out of the bar for him when he needed to sit down while making his way in.

It broke my heart to see my father like this. I couldn't understand how Bea could take him out in dirty old clothes and wave people over to the table to visit with him. He was always such a proud man. I think if he had been clean and in clean clothes, I could have handled it better. But he looked and smelled dirty. There was thick, black grime under his nails. His clothes were full of stains and dirt and didn't fit. He had big pieces of elastic crudely sewn into the back of his trousers—which I'm sure was the work of dear Miriam, trying to protect him—but the clothes were so old they needed to be burnt, not made to fit. She was keeping him in smelly old rags while she was always well dressed. Didn't she see that others could see the state he was in ?

I was, because of my on-going battle with Hep C, still having financial troubles at the time of this trip. I didn't have enough money to live on. I had begged Dad and Bea in letters to let me come home. I could move in and help take care of Dad. Bea said that wasn't a possibility and that I needed to have the government take care of me. She said my father had no money and she was not going to let me steal any more of what he had. She said Dale Bandel and I had been stealing his money, and that's why she had to move Dad's account to US Trust. Not even bothering to pretend now that Dad had made this move with his money but that she had !

Conversations with this woman during my visit were insane. Dad kept saying, "She is my only daughter! I want to help her. Bea, isn't there anyway I can help her?"

Bea would scream back, "I am your only wife!"

I asked Bea if her heart was made of stone or ice. How could she not help me with money or a roof over my head? I was begging and crying. I wanted Dad to continue to pay Nick's tuition as he used to, because I had had to take out a huge loan for Nick to be in school that year.

Bea said, "Nick is a man. He is a man. He must get a job. The government can take care of you! Your daddy has no money. You must go to the government!"

Dad asked why I couldn't stay in the house. I had been trying not to get into anything with him and save him from a scene with Bea, but now I told him, "Bea called before I came and told me that under no circumstances was I allowed to be alone with you."

Bea immediately started screaming, "She's a liar. She is a liar. I told you she was a liar."

Dad looked at me once again with that sheepish look and said, "I don't think that helped your case too much."

Bea suggested that Dad could take out a loan that I would repay when I got any inheritance. She rather stunningly suggested a loan for $100k. Bea helped Dad call US Trust and talk to James Dowling, who was VP in charge of loans. Bea then left the room, saying, "George does not need me to do this."

Dad had a very hard time talking to Mr. Dowling. He asked me to take the phone and explain what Dowling was saying. Dowling told

Dad how much the payments per month would be on $100k. I think it was something like $325 per month. Dad said he could afford that and asked the man to draw up the papers and I would come in and get them. I drove to US Trust and picked up the papers. They told me that my father's signature alone would not be sufficient, that Bea had to sign them, too. I asked why, since it was Dad's money? I was told for the first time that it was actually "their" money. Bea had arranged it so that she had actually become a co-owner of the account.

Stunned, I went back to the house with the paperwork. As I came in the door, Bea grabbed the papers out of my hand and said, "What is this? I will never sign this! You have conned your father! How did you make him do this?"

I said, "Bea, you were the one who suggested $100,000."

Bea sat me down and made me go over what I owed and what I needed money for. I did this repeatedly, but she couldn't make the figures add up, strangely slow in her ability to understand what I was saying.

She told me to leave the house and that she and Dad would discuss it and let me know the next day what they decided. I went to Nellie's with a heavy heart; I knew I was probably not going to get a dime. I had no idea what I was going to do next. My options had pretty much run out.

This was the first time the reality of where I was in my life hit me. All my life I had been told that when Dad died I would be very well off. That I had nothing to worry about. I would be a very wealthy woman. I had heard this from Dad, lawyers and bankers my entire life. I wish no one had ever told me that because I would have lived my life in an entirely different way if I had known what really was to come.

§

The next day, I met Dad and Bea for lunch at the B&T again. Today Dad, on his own, without Bea ordering for him, asked for two iced coffees, not the vodka Bea had ordered for him the previous days.

He was much more animated. I asked him about the loan, and he told me to come back to the house after lunch. When I did, he told me I was to get $30k, not $100. This at least would cover my current debts, but I would have no money to live on afterward. Bea said that was too bad; it was the best they could do.

Bea kept telling my father that they were broke. They didn't have enough money to feed him or pay for his medical care, and there was no way they could help me. She would never have been able to mount arguments like this if Dad had had all his marbles. I took the signed papers to US Trust and they then wired the money a few days later to my Key Bank account. Afterward, I went back to Nellie's. Relieved to be out of hot water for now.

Unexpectedly, my father called Nellie's and asked, "Would you and Nellie like to have dinner with us at the Golf Terrace at the Everglades Club tonight?" After the way the week had gone this was a stunning invitation.

Nellie told me she would only do it for my sake, because she hated idea of having to spend a dinner with Bea. I asked Dad if he had taken a nap and he said no, but that he felt good and didn't need a nap. I realized he was awake and alert because he had had iced coffee at lunch instead of vodka. What a difference!

Nellie and I met Dad and Bea at the Everglades. Dad had a terrible time ordering. He kept asking the waiter for the real menu, the one with the prices on it. The waiter kept saying, "That is what you have, Mr. Ford."

The prices were written out, and Dad could not understand it. He also didn't like the big heavy leather cover of the menu and wanted a paper menu. Bea did nothing to help him. I tried to help him order, but in the end, he only ordered a crab cake appetizer. Afterward, he was still hungry. Bea ignored him and kept trying to talk to Nellie about parties Nellie couldn't give a damn about.

At one point in the dinner, Dad picked up a lemon wedge wrapped in a doily cover to prevent it from squirting one when you squeezed it. Dad put it in his mouth - I guess he thought it was a muffin - and tried to take a bite out of it. By the time I realized what he was doing, it was too late. He made all kinds of faces and kept looking at the lemon, not understanding. Under any other circumstances, it might have been funny.

We had a nice dinner anyway. Bea kept talking to Nellie, so Dad didn't say too much. I was able to get Dad to the dessert table to have a nice desert since he hadn't had much to eat for dinner. At the end of the night, as we were leaving, Dad took a left at the front door instead of going through it and accidentally walked into a broom closet. He stood there with this shocked look on his face and I went over to him and led him out the real door.

It was very clear that Dad was not in charge of anything anymore. It had been a long time since he had been, but this visit made it abundantly clear. Dad had no idea what was going on, and Bea made damn sure things stayed that way.

My father prided himself on his grooming, and he would have hated his dirty clothes and nails. Bea told me that he couldn't get in the tub anymore, so he just splashed water on himself. After I told her something had to be done, Miriam was called in to give him a bath. Miriam got soaking wet trying to get him into the tub. Who knows how long it had been since he had been able to bathe himself. I sent Bea advertisements for bathtubs with doors and showers with seats bath, but she never did anything about it.

Before I went to the airport, I went to the house to say goodbye and found that Dad was having a failing spell. He had become very weak and could not walk. Bea went to the garage and got an old, rusty wheelchair, and I put him in it. He wanted to go to the bathroom and couldn't manage it himself, so I lifted him on and off the john. Then I helped him back into the wheelchair and into his bed.

Meanwhile, Bea called the doctor in a panic. (Strangely, she called a doctor at Mass General in Boston, rather than a local doctor in Palm Beach, which I couldn't understand.) The doctor asked if Dad had taken his medication. Bea said she didn't know, that he kept all his pills in the bathroom and took all the labels off them. I asked to speak to the doctor. He explained that Dad probably just needed his medications, and that Bea had to be made to give them to him and not let Dad dispense them himself. Bea picked up the other line and started talking over him.

He said, "Please let me speak to Mr. Ford's daughter." Bea said, "No, doctor. I am his wife, and I must be on the phone." I wanted to stay, but Bea told me to leave. She said she would call me if he didn't improve. I called from the airport and then again from Atlanta, and Dad was on the phone by then, sounding much better, so I guess the proper medication did the trick.

I left Palm Beach with a heavy heart. I expected that I might not see Dad again. I took a mental picture of him when I hugged him, lying helpless in his bed, to say goodbye. I called the day after I returned home, and Miriam put me through to my father. I told him I had arrived safe and sound and that I loved him and missed him very much. He told me he loved me too and wished I was there. So did I but I was told by my lawyers that Bea was his wife and in that position I was only his daughter which gave me little if no rights at all. At least while he was alive. There was nothing to be done!

I couldn't get through to my father again for the rest of the winter. I continued to send letters, cards, and newspaper clippings about sailing and riding and everything he enjoyed. I doubt he ever saw them. I sent Bea books on dealing with the elderly. My wonderful friends, realizing how much trouble I was in, took care of me. They knew I was alone in the world, except for my son, who was in the last semester of college that I would be able to pay for.

§

May 10, 2004, was Dad's ninety-seventh birthday. I put together a letter and a list of ninety-seven memories we had shared. I had no idea whether he would see it. I cried whenever I wrote to him, and this occasion was even sadder still. I missed him so much. I wanted to be with him, and I was not even allowed phone time with him. I was heartbroken. I knew he missed me, too. He always told me to come see him and had a hard time understanding why I wasn't there. Many times, to avoid hurting him or upsetting him, I wouldn't tell him that Bea had said I was not welcome. I would just say that it wasn't going to work out, or make some other innocuous comment. Trying as hard as I could I tried repeatedly to get through to Dad on the phone to wish him a Happy Birthday. I left message after message but to no avail.

A few days after his birthday, Bea called and said, "It is my duty to inform you that your father has second stage metastasized melanoma, and the doctor says he will live only three to six months." She also told me he was sundowning, which I later learned meant, "Becoming agitated at dusk."

I said I would come right away. She said that wouldn't be necessary. I decided to come anyway. I demanded to know the name of Dad's doctors. Amazingly she gave them to me. I called Dr. Ness and Dr. Jacobson, and they told me Dad was not at death's door and that my plan, to arrive in a few weeks, early June would be fine.

Dr. Ness asked whether I could get nursing help for my father. He said that he had sent over many health care workers, but they all kept being fired. He had told Bea to call hospice and get someone in to help care for Dad. He told me on the phone in May and again in June when I went to see him that Bea had not yet called hospice. In fact they were not called and they did not come in to take care of my father until the last week of his life the following December—six months later. Bea did not want anyone around him that might offer real help. To isolate him from his family was cruel, but Bea isolated him from proper medical care because she didn't want him alone with anyone who could drive a car, dial a phone, or witness what was happening to him. Bea only thought she was safe if it was just she and Miriam in the house.

I thought Bea would soften about letting me in the house since Dad was obviously in his last days. I wrote an e-mail asking to stay in the house. She countered with an e-mail purportedly from my father saying it would be inconvenient for me to stay there. The entire time I was there, Dad kept asking, "Why are you leaving? Why don't you stay here?" This time I answered that Bea would not allow me.

I visited him every day. I was allowed in from eleven in the morning until four in the afternoon. Then I had to leave. Bea said she didn't want me to see him "sundowning". I thought this was just crazy, but I deferred to her because I didn't want to get Dad upset any more then he was by my not being allowed to stay in the house. On the last night I was there, Bea, evidently feeling claustrophobic, asked if I wanted to go with them for an early dinner to a little fish restaurant on Dixie, just over the Southern Blvd. Bridge. I said I would love to. We pulled up right outside, and I helped Dad in. He could barely walk and preferred the wheelchair at this point but I got him through the door.

Dad's condition was bad, as he was a very old man. He was obviously senile and very weak. Amazingly, he looked younger than his ninety-seven years, but his was white and quite long. It had been a long time since he had seen a barber. (the hairdresser who last saw him told me after Dad died that he had gone over once that last winter to cut his hair. He said he felt sorry for Dad because he was so dirty and smelled so bad) His fingernails were terribly long. Because he'd been sedentary, his stomach was so big that he didn't have any pants that could close. Someone had ripped out the back of his pants and put in elastic so that he could zip up the front, but now even, this wasn't enough to be able for him to close them.

Dad kept asking, "Weezie, don't I have any pants that close?"

I asked Bea, and she said I could look in his closet, that maybe the blue pair might fit.

Nothing fit him - not one pair. Everything in his closet was so old and filthy dirty.

I asked Bea, "Why don't we put him in pajamas? At least with the elastic waist they would be more comfortable and give him a little dignity."

Bea replied, "No pajamas—otherwise they'll be dirty for tonight."

I couldn't believe Dad had only one pair of pajamas. I announced that I was going to Wal-Mart to buy him pants with elastic waists. "He cannot sit around in ratty, filthy old pants that don't fit. He needs something clean and comfortable."

Bea freaked out. "No! Don't buy him anything. I've ordered pants for him, and they'll be here next week."

(At his funeral, I would see a photo of Dad at Thanksgiving, a month before he died, taken by Bea's sister. He looked like he was seething with anger in it. His hair was very long and white, flowing down over his shoulders, and his stomach was hanging out of his pants. Bea never did get him anything to wear that fit him.)

Dad asked me if I could cut his fingernails. I told him I would be happy to and went to his bathroom for clippers. A year and a half after I had made such a stink about Dad having a bathtub he could get into, nothing had been done. Bea's meanness and cruelty toward this poor old man who had allowed her to have the life she wanted was criminal. It made me ill.

I cut Dad's fingernails, which were bordering on Howard Hughes's (although not actually seeing Howard Hughes perhaps they were as bad or worse!) This made Dad happy. He asked me to get a nail file and he kept filing his fingernails. He kept a comb and the file next to him on the table by his chair. He liked to comb his hair, and there was plenty of it to comb now.

Dad's doctor, Dr. Ness, and I had talked extensively before my arrival and after I was in town, and he felt that my father did not know what he was doing at all. I had asked if he was Bea's doctor, too. He said he was. I said, "She has been pretty loopy for years. Is she all right to take care of him?"

Dr Ness, who is from Maine, had replied, in a term used in Maine regularly I have been told, " Mrs. Ford is squirrelly."

Because I knew from Dr. Ness that Dad had an appointment with him that week I asked Bea if he was going to see his Dr any time while I was there. She told me Dad was seeing Dr. Ness in a few days, and I said I would love to go along. Dad said he would like me to be there. I had to call Dr. Ness and his assistant, who I had become good friends with by then, while trying to help them get Dad the medical care they knew he needed, to tell them they had to act as if they didn't know me.

Dr. Ness said, "Mr. Ford, you are taking Alzheimer's drugs. Have you ever had a memory test?"

Bea answered for him, "Yes, I think his previous doctor gave him one."

Miriam later told me she'd been with them for the earlier test, which Dad failed.

Dr Ness said since he was new to Dad's case, being his doctor only since November 2003, when they came back from Newport, and Dad's previous doctor had retired, he wanted to do the test again, in case some other medication could help. My father said that was happy to do this. Dr. Ness gave Dad his test. I think he scored 16, an extremely low score. It was sad. My father had been a brilliant engineer, and he was now unable to sign his name or know what year it was or what city we were in.

After giving Dad the test Dr. Ness agreed easily with Mike Simon's advice that I get in touch with Jamie Pressley and help him enact Dad's trust. I didn't know yet that Bea was a trustee and I was not. I thought it was still Bea, the bank, and me—the way it had been all of my life. I wrote a letter to US Trust, saying that they needed to step in. Dad was not being well cared for, and I didn't know where else to turn. I had a very nice phone call from Sue Capodanno, the head of the trust department. She was very understanding and promised to go to the house and check on him. She didn't. Gary Lickle would do this in August almost two months later. The visit from Gary was the last one my father had from anyone who spoke English.

§

During this last week long visit with my father, June 2004, Miriam and I began our communications. One day, she came up to me when I was walking through the living room to the kitchen to get my father a glass of water. She stuck a little note in my pocket, said to call her at six o'clock, and scurried away. I went into the kitchen and looked at the note. She had put her phone number on it. I went back to Dad's room and gave him his water. I was more than curious to hear what Miriam had to say.

At four PM, when I was told I had to leave, I went back to my friend Stuart Howard-Smith's house, where I was staying, and waited nervously until six PM. I rang, Miriam and her daughter Maria got on the phone and said her mother would like to meet with me. We agreed to meet in half an hour. At 6:30 PM, I arrived in the Havana Restaurant parking lot. Miriam and her two daughters, Maria and Carolina, were there. I got out of my car and asked if they would like to go inside and get a cup of coffee. Miriam said no, she was too scared of Bea and her brothers Fernando and Louis. One of them could see us. She said she was afraid for her life. Bea and her family were Colombians, and she thought they might kill her. I suggested we sit in my rented car, which no one would recognize. Miriam thought that would be okay.

We got in the car and Miriam told me she saw me cutting my father's fingernails and could see how much I loved him. She said it brought tears to her eyes. She said Mrs. Bea never touched him. Mrs. Bea called him a smelly old man and wouldn't have anything to do with him. She told me that Bea and her entire family had been plotting for years to take Dad's money away from Nick and me. They would do anything to keep Nicky and me from seeing any of it. It would all go to Bea and her family in the end. She told me that Bea constantly called her lawyer, Faxon Henderson, to be coached on how to achieve this.

Miriam told me she had pieces of paper taken from the house that would prove Bea had manipulated my father for years. She thought I should get his money since I was his daughter and I obviously loved him, and that Bea, who treated him so badly, didn't deserve a thing.

After I left, Miriam and I stayed in touch over the phone. She would have her daughter Carolina call me, at the island over the summer to let me know that I could talk to my father. She had Carolina call because she was nervous about calling the island from Dad's phone. She was afraid of Bea and knew there would be hell to pay if her connection to me were found out. Seeing the island phone number on Dad's phone bill would sink this operation instantly.

Most of the summer, I was unable to get through on the phone. Miriam told me that because I was in the USA, Bea was afraid I would show up and take my father to the bank. So Bea spent most of the summer during banking hours sitting in the house, even though I was 1500 miles away. Because of this her phone screening method was back in full swing.

§

At the end of August, Hurricane Francis was bearing down on Palm Beach, and I knew Palm Beach was to be evacuated. I left three messages sternly saying, "Bea, I know you have to evacuate. I need to know where you are taking my father and what is going on."

She finally called me back and told me she had booked a suite at a hotel at the West Palm Beach airport and that Miriam would be with them. The West Palm Beach airport is just over the bridge and still close to the ocean and the full brunt of the storm. I told her she should drive to Sarasota, to her sister's place, but she refused. She didn't want to put up with Dad in the car for that long.

Dad, Bea and Miriam spent four or five days in the hotel - sleeping one night on chairs in the hallway, while the wind howled and the windows blew out all over the building. The day after the storm was over, my old friend Mark Howard-Smith went to the hotel to check on them and to see if they needed anything. Mark told me that Bea said Dad was asleep and he was unable to see him, and the bedroom door was shut.

They had no electricity in the time they were there. They were on the eighth floor, and they were virtually trapped up there because they couldn't get Dad down because the elevators didn't work. Miriam was sent down the eight flights of stairs daily to get supplies for both my father and Bea and she had to climb back up those stairs carrying them when she returned.

Finally, the hotel was hooked up to a generator and they got him out. They drove down to Boca Raton, and the three of them—Bea, Dad, and Miriam—stayed with Bea's brother Fernando in his tiny apartment. Fernando had Miriam clean his house and do his laundry "since she was there." Poor Miriam didn't see her family for two weeks. A tree fell on her car during the storm, and she asked Bea to repair it since she had stayed with Dad for all this time without a break. Bea refused.

(After Dad died Miriam sued Bea for $29,000 + for back wages, time and a half for overtime etc because she had her working 24/7 for most of the last months of his life. Away from her own family, husband and daughters and only paid her normal 5 day a week wage. Miriam won every penny Bea legally owed her. One small triumph for a woman who richly deserved all of that and more.)

I tried to call every day during the time of the storm, and I called Bea's cell one time right after they arrived at Fernando's. Bea didn't always answer. I am sure she was screening, using the caller ID. But she did put Dad on the cell phone a couple of times. My conversations with him were all one-sided, like talking to a small child or worse, because he didn't volunteer anything. One of these times when we were finished talking and I had said good bye, Dad just put the phone down. I assume he didn't know how to close the little flip cell phone that Bea had given him. I could hear Bea and Fernando jabbering away in Spanish. I had just been given a glimpse of my father's life. My poor Daddy, with a minimal grasp of reality under the best of circumstances, was surrounded by people talking in what to him must have sounded like gibberish. No wonder he was slipping away so quickly. Without any mental or physical activity, it must have been like being in an insane asylum.

Fernando finally found them an assisted living apartment, since the house was too badly damaged from the storm to return to it, or so Bea said. They moved to a tiny two-bedroom apartment off Okeechobee, almost to the turnpike. This is where Dad spent his last days, in an alien place with alien-sounding people.

The last time I had a conversation with him was the day after the election in November. Dad and I had always had fabulous political discussions, and I wanted to talk to him about the outcome of the election. Dad had worked for every Republican candidate for President all his life. He had organized Industry for Eisenhower and worked in campaigns for Nixon, Goldwater, Reagan, and so on. He worked extensively with Nelson Rockefeller his first two terms as Governor of New York. I knew he would be or at least should be interested in the presidential election. I told him about Bush's victory and that the Republican Party had control of the House and the Senate for the first time since 1932. He wasn't too sure of all that I was talking about, maybe not any of what I was talking about, but he enjoyed it. At the end of this conversation, our last, as it turned out, he said, "Come soon. Stay long." I am still heartbroken that I was unable to fulfill this last request.

I don't think I will ever get over the pain of him wanting me there and my not being able to be with him. I run through my head, repeatedly, all the "what ifs" and "I should have's". I should have lived closer to him; I should have forced my way into the house. What if I had actually showed up on the doorstep with my bag? With Dad right there, would she have thrown me out? I will never know, and I will always feel I let him down when he was weak and needed me, but Mike Simon had advised me that showing up would only make a scene. She would be liable to call the police to have me removed and that wouldn't help anything.

I tried to call him for two days on my birthday, December 5, but Miriam's daughter told me that Bea had said all phone activity was being recorded, and that Miriam had better not try to put me through to my father. Whether Bea was recording or not, I have no idea, but her saying so worked, because Miriam was afraid to put me on the line with him, even though she was alone with him in that little apartment all day. (Bea spent her days at the PB house overseeing the workers working on the hurricane damage, which I guess was extensive.)

Miriam told me during one of my conversations with her, after Dad died, that Bea had been sent a check from the insurance company for Two hundred thousand dollars and that Bea danced around the house while her husband lay dying, saying she was the luckiest woman in the world because all this money had just come her way. She was never going to be poor again and that she had fought hard to get all that she had.

Bea called me on December 19, the Sunday before Christmas, and told me that Dr. Jacobson (the cancer Doctor) said Dad was going, but it would be a month or two before he died. I wanted to come right away, but she told me the doctor said I should wait until after Christmas.

I should have called Dr. Jacobson, but I didn't. I do not know why I didn't and why, after all I had been through with her, I actually believed Bea. I booked tickets for Nick and me to arrive January 1st, believing we had plenty of time. Since Dad's house was all torn up by the hurricane, and since all my friends had their own families staying in their homes over the holidays, we had no place to stay, which contributed to my justifying the delay.

On Christmas Eve December 24th 2004 at 1:30 PM GMT, in London, Bea called and said, "Weezie, your Daddy is dying. Can you come right away?"

I replied "Of course, but the next flight I can get will be tomorrow morning."

I made frantic phone calls to BA. It took about two hours to get things organized, and I called Bea back to tell her we were arriving the next day. When I called, Bea answered and said in a cold voice, "It's too late. He just died."

To add insult to injury I had taken my black suit to the cleaners too so that it would be ready to go when I headed down to Palm Beach to be with my father before he died. I raced around the corner to the dry cleaners and in front of the door were the two women that worked in there locking up. I ran up to them and said please can you open the door and get my suit. My father has just died and I must have it to go to the funeral. I was stunned when they refused saying that the shop was closed and they would not reopen it. I pleaded with them and neither of them ever even said they were sorry. They just said no we are closed. Come back in two days when we reopen. Talk about adding insult to injury.

Bea said she would tell US Trust to give me the money for the tickets. She didn't. I had to talk fast to get them to organize a "loan" for me to get there. Nothing was ever going to be easy for me I was soon to find out.

Chapter 6
The Aftermath of Loss:
Palm Beach, London, Palm Beach

We arrived on Christmas Day on a British Airways flight into Miami. As our 747 was landing, just as we were about to touch the ground, the engines roared, and up we went into the air again. There was another plane still on the runway. If you have never felt a 747 shift gears like this and rumble off, you haven't lived. Anyway, Nick and I arrived in Miami and went to Avis, where I was told that my US driver's license had been revoked because I had not paid a speeding ticket in NY State. I actually thought I had paid it! Nick was under twenty-five, so we couldn't rent a car. We ended up taking a Yellow Cab from Miami all the way to our friend Stuart's house. It was just a dreadful day. It seemed nothing like Christmas. To top it all off when we got there Stuart was home in bed with the flu!

The following day we arranged to meet Bea, who brought Fernando with her, at the funeral home. This was the first time I had seen her since my last visit 6 months before and she made sure I was not a part of the planning for the funeral. Everything had been done without ever discussing anything with me. Why I kept deluding myself into thinking that I mattered at all at this point is beyond me. But I did.

We also arranged to meet with Miriam in the Publix grocery store parking lot that same day. Once again, we met with her in the car with her two daughters. She brought with her the three pieces of paper she took out of the wastepaper basket in Bea's study. They were "scripts" for Dad to read so he could instruct Jamie Pressley on changes to be made to Dad's documents. They were hand written by Bea in large writing so Dad would tell "Jimmy" Pressley to eliminate Nicholas George "Grand." (Nick's last name is Grant, and she should have written "Jamie Pressley.") There were four of these sheets of paper and I have included a couple of them at the end of the book.

Miriam also brought us a tape recording of Bea screaming at my father and threatening to have him taken away. She said she recorded it about two or three weeks before he died. Bea was screaming at him because he climbed into her bed by mistake.

Bea kept screeching, "Do you want them to take you away?"

Dad's tiny pleading voice was answering pleading, "No, no."

"They will take you away!"

"No, no."

"They will take you away to the hospital."

"No, no, no, no."

Nick and I sobbed. It was too much. Miriam had recorded this conversation because "Mrs. Bea" was always yelling at my poor father. She couldn't stand it anymore, and she thought someone should hear it. Miriam went into that apartment with an old fashioned cassette recorder that you pushed the buttons on and they made a loud click. She did this with it in her purse risking Bea hearing the noise. Miriam was so brave to have done this.

§

At the funeral home, Bea's brother Louie, a retired doctor, told Nick and I that Dr. Jacobson had told Bea on Dec 4 that Dad could go at any time. Not only did Bea never bother to let me know, but December 5th was my birthday and I had tried repeatedly on that day to get through to him on the phone. I am sure she wanted to make sure I wasn't there and waited until the last minute so I couldn't be able to be there. I think he was dead when she called me the first time, as she was hysterical during that phone call. By the time I got reservations, he had been gone for a while, so she had recovered to her icy normal self. She masterminded her control over our relationship, doing everything she could to keep us apart. Her cruelty knew no bounds.

The funeral was uncomfortable for Nick and me. Bea took care of everything before we arrived. She had his obituary written; amazingly, it was mostly right, though she added some stuff in there that just wasn't true. The most glaring untruth was the headline in the Palm Beach Shiny Sheet, which Dale Bandel laughed whole heartedly at it read "Philanthropist George E. Ford Dies." Dale better than anyone knew this was truly rewriting history. Dad was not philanthropic in the least—unless it was for something like the Ruffed Grouse Society of North America, which he was president of for a time.

Bea made all the funeral arrangements, not consulting me on about anything. She purchased a $10,000 brass coffin for Dad and was having a $98,000 mausoleum in a Catholic cemetery in West Palm Beach. My father was never a Catholic; he didn't practice any religion, although he was raised Presbyterian, like his Scottish ancestors.

Before Dad died, he had asked me three times where I was going to be buried. I told him I wanted to be cremated so I could be put in a little box in the ground at the island with our old dog Boo. He said he would very much like to go there, too. Every few years for the last ten years or so, he told me again that was what he wanted. Dale Bandel told me that he'd said spending money on even a pine box was too much.

When I saw the coffin before the funeral, I was horrified; it was a burnt copper color with big, gold-colored handles—very obviously metal. The night before the funeral, there was a visiting hour at the funeral home with the casket. They asked if they should open it, but I didn't want to see my poor old Daddy the way I knew he would look. It is the only thing that Bea let me decide. That evening, while waiting out the stream of people paying their respects, Gloria, Bea's sister, handed me a photograph taken at Thanksgiving of my father with her, Bea, and Fernando standing around him in a wheelchair. I asked to keep the photo, as it was the last one taken of my father, and Gloria said okay. Then Bea took her aside to tell her something. Gloria told me she would like the photo back, promising to send me a copy once she got home. A copy never arrived. The photo really showed the terrible, unkempt state Bea had kept my father in. It would have told this entire tale if I had it now to put in this book!

Before we left for the funeral the next morning, Bea went up to the coffin and knelt, as if she were praying. Since this woman never went to church this was hard to buy. I am sure if she was praying it was to be able to keep this poor old man's money. And praying that so far secret marriage previous to marrying my father never comes to light.

I waited respectfully for the grieving widow to finish and then I went up to the metal box myself, and started tapping my fingernails on it. It was made of something that felt and sounded like tin. Knowing that my father would never have let a moment like this go by without some frivolity to lighten the mood, as I tapped it, I said, "Hello, Daddy, are you in there? Just wanted to tell you that I loved you very much and will miss you every day for the rest of my life."

Bea and her family stared at me in shock, their jaws hanging wide open.

We left to go to the funeral, and I have no recollection of who rode with whom, but Nick and I did not let go of each other the entire time. We held each other's hands tight. I was reminded of the way Dad had held my hand a few years before, on the night Bea threw a dinner dance that she told Dad was their anniversary party, even though their anniversary was February 16, months before the May party. It was actually an anniversary party for Bea's brother Louis and his wife Amita - paid for by Dad. I don't remember any friends of my father's there or any Palm Beachers at all. The back garden was full of Colombians from Miami. It was quite a big party with an orchestra playing allot of rhumba. Dad took hold of my hand and never let it go the entire night. My friend Katy Keiffer and I sat at a table on either side of him; no one else even bothered to talk to him. It wouldn't have mattered, because everyone in the party spoke Spanish. Even Bea didn't bother with him as she was having the time of her life dancing away with her brother Fernando and all his gay friends.

We got to the Poinciana Chapel, since Dad didn't have a church and Bea was not a practicing Catholic. This was a nondenominational chapel. Bea physically pushed Nick and me into the second and she then ushered her family into the front row. Nick's grandmother, Micky Grant, Wayne's mother, saw this, came up front, and sat with Nick and me, which was incredibly sweet and understanding. It meant a great deal to me that she was there. A few of my other friends came up and hugged me sitting in the pew when they saw what had happened.

Nick read the piece he had chosen beautifully but with a quivering voice. When he sat down, he took my program and with a little pencil wrote, "She sheds no tears." I couldn't have said it better.

I had prepared a little piece that I had written on the plane. I worked up all my strength and read it through my tears:

> Regardless of how you try and make sense of a loved one's death, it's always too soon, too fast, too impossible to comprehend, and we are left bereft, wondering if there were anything we could have done to change the outcome. There is never a good time; it's always the worst time, and it is always far too soon. Even after my father's long life, it doesn't seem possible that he is no longer with us.

My father had above all else a wonderful sense of humor and fun. And I know that he would not want us to be heavy hearted today, but go on, as if he was still with us. We all know he is here, in our hearts, forever. I am sure if he were here, he would have something amusing to say about all of this done on his behalf. My father was not in the least bit ostentatious and always wanted to impart in me humility. He always sang to me, and I am sure he would have made up a little song and a funny face to make me laugh today.

Dad leaves us with a memory of a great outdoorsman who loved life, his family, and his friends. The more laughs we could have, the better. He lived his life as if it was meant to be enjoyed. That is not to say Dad didn't have a serious side. He certainly did. He was always sincere, honest, and correct. He made sure that I was always on time!

Dad was born in Barrie, Ontario, but moved to Rochester, to live with his aunt and uncle at the age of twelve, when his parents died in the flu epidemic in 1917 and 1919. He was an avid student of American history. He was the embodiment of the true American dream. He managed, through hard work and the help of my mother, to build a prosperous business.

I was born to parents who in those days were quite old. Dad was forty-eight and my mother was thirty-eight. They had been married fourteen years before I came along. By the time I arrived, they had carved out a wonderful life that revolved around two months of skiing at the Lake Placid Club and Top Notch in Stowe in the winter, bone fishing in the Bahamas in the spring, sailing and salmon fishing in the summers, and upland bird hunting every fall. There was also time for skeet every Sunday, as well as horseback riding and golf. Daddy, did I forget anything?

Dad's love for the outdoors was his greatest gift. I can weather anything on the back of a horse, skiing in some spectacular location, or just being on Grindstone Island, our lifelong family paradise.

So many things about Dad I recognize in myself and in Nicky, who inherited his quick wit and strong conservative beliefs. No memories of my father would be complete without mentioning his proud, conservative patriotism. This summer I was able to watch Ronald Reagan's funeral with my Dad. He wasn't always tracking what was going on, but he remembered what a good man President Reagan had been. I found myself crying through a good deal of the television coverage. For me, Ronald Reagan and my father were cut from the same cloth. They had both come from modest means, and having lived through two world wars and the Depression they were gentleman of the finest order. They lived by the edicts of honesty, hard work, decency, and humor. The Greatest Generation, as Tom Brokaw so eloquently called them.

I could not have asked for a better father. I learned from him when Mom died how to survive great loss. He was an expert on the subject, having lost both his parents at a young age. When my mother died, he was always there for me. I was very lucky to spend the first fifty years of my life knowing his strength was there if I needed him. He showed me that I could weather any storm. It is incomprehensible to me that I will not have his strong, loving support.

Nicky and I will miss you, dear Daddy. We will love and cherish you for as long as we live. May you rest in eternal peace and find true happiness in heaven with friends and family you have loved and now welcome you home.

After the service, there was a reception at the Everglades Club. Gary Lickle, no longer president of US Trust, took me aside and said, "Don't worry, Weezie. It's over; we will make sure you are well taken care of." Gary is 6 ft 7 inches, and I always find talking to him difficult if we are standing, but he made me sigh in relief. Oh how I wanted to wallow in that feeling that had become so foreign to me.

Once the "party" was over, we drove out to the cemetery on Southern Blvd., where Bea was taking Dad. When we got there, they took the casket to a wall of drawers and pushed it across the gravelly cement into an open bottom drawer. It made an awful noise.

I couldn't stand it. This was a dreadful scene, far from anything my father would have wanted for himself, and the ceremony with the drawer was the end for me.

I said, "I can't stand this," and Nick and I, already holding hands, again, walked to a bench about a hundred yards from this scene. After they sealed him in, Bea came to show me where the mausoleum she was having built was going. I told her it was all awful; she knew that this was not what Dad would have wanted.

§

The funeral was on Jan 31, 2004—New Year's Eve. At the time, I had no idea what day it was. I was in the fog between a death and a funeral, but since it was on a weekend, Nick and I needed to go somewhere where I felt like I was at home and loved. We got into the car and drove to Naples to stay with Junie Howard-Smith Augsbury and her husband Frank, the woman who, along with Patty Bain from Juniper Island, is more my mother than anyone else alive.

All I wanted to do was sleep and lie in the sun by her pool. Which is exactly what we did. On Sunday, we drove back to Palm Beach.

At the funeral, I asked Bea if she wanted to have lunch on Monday when I got back, and she said yes. I rang her on Monday morning, and she said, "I do not want to meet with you again," and hung up the phone. That was the last time Bea and I ever spoke. She had her lawyer contact mine to tell him that under no circumstances was I to contact her.

§

The following day, Tuesday, January 4, the reading of the will was scheduled for Nick and me to attend. Bea was not going to be there. She didn't need to be; after all, she had written the whole thing. This second part of my father's passing was even weirder than the one before. Two days after we'd come back from our decompression chamber in Naples, Nick and I had this meeting with all the lawyers.

Bea had Dad take the houses in Palm Beach and Newport out of the trust and changed the trust so that I was no longer a trustee. Before that, it had always been Dale Bandel, me, and Bea as trustees. I had known that once she had the money away from Dale, I would be out of the loop, but I didn't know she had removed me as a trustee.

This is the first time I heard Bea's birthday was May 19th. I told the lawyers they must be wrong, that her birthday was in March, that she was a Pisces.

Nick said, "Yes she has a huge Lalique Pisces fish in the middle of the living room."

The lawyer said again that her driver's license said May 19, 1928. At the time, I just shook my head because I had such a hard time digesting what these people were telling me. The discrepancy in birth dates took a back seat. Previously, the money Dad left me outright to live on until Bea's death had now been put into a trust that Bea, US Trust, and Gary Lickle were trustees of. That money was never supposed to be in a trust, but there it was. Now, both houses had been taken out of the trust and willed separately to Bea alone. The money that Bea was to live on until she died, when it was to come back to me, was now in trust with the same three trustees—Bea, Gary, and US Trust.

For thirty years, until the last four years of Dad's life, the will had been that I would have a nice amount of money outright when he died, with the houses and the money in the bank in a trust for Bea's lifetime, with Bea, Dale Bandel, and me as trustees. It was to come to me when Bea died to be in a trust with Dale and me as trustees and Nicky as the remainder-man. Nick would have received it all once I died, with the trust dissolving. We learned at that meeting that in the last four years of Dad's life, there had been five major changes to his testamentary documents. The weaker he got, the more Bea had him change. Until in the end she basically had it all for herself.

Under the new terms, I had some money, but it was all on her whim. Gary Lickle and US Trust were her agents. Dad had lived long enough for her to take complete control. When Nick and I walked out of this meeting, I felt as if I had gone ten rounds with Mohammed Ali. First, we lived through years of being kept away from my father. After all the viciousness I endured, I had to suffer this. We had been forced into a battle, and this was not the way Dad would have wanted it. I hadn't wanted it this way, either.

Dad seemed to have held on to one bit of his wits, because for a short time he had appointed Nick—who was all of nineteen at the time—as trustee. I am sure that Bea put her foot down and said in no way was Weezie going to be a trustee, handling her—Bea's—money.

I think Dad or his lawyer must have said, "Okay, then let's make Nick a trustee at least keeping it in his family if you remove Weezie." But that didn't last long.

Miriam later gave me papers that she removed from Bea's wastepaper basket, and in Bea's handwriting, oversized so that my father could read it, I read, "Eliminate Nicholas George Grant. Replace with Brad Greer." (see attached*) Miriam told me that this was a "script" that she told Dad to read to Jamie Pressley, who would then draw up papers doing so. I can only assume that Brad Greer for whatever reason was unavailable to become trustee or perhaps he was uncomfortable with it having been Dale Bandels boss for years and knowing full well this was not what Dad had wanted. So he had in the end been replaced by Gary Lickle.

Miriam also gave a ten-page statement just in case she went back to Central America or was otherwise unavailable. It made for chilling reading. First, Miriam detailed Dad's worsening senility: he lost interest in reading the newspaper, a lifelong habit; he no longer recognized her; he would look outside and tell Miriam what the New York weather was. Second, she talked about Bea's growing mistreatment of Dad: she screamed at him and threatened him; he would get so frustrated that he spit on the floor because he had no power left to do anything else. Third, Miriam talked about my relationship with Dad: he called me "a good, good daughter"; Bea prevented Dad from talking to me on the phone; she told him I was "lying" about my illness and tried to prevent him from paying my expenses; Dad kept telling Bea that the house was Weezie's. She detailed Bea's increasing attempts to manipulate Dad and take over his money. Bea would say the car was broken when Dad wanted to go to the bank; she wrote "scripts" for Dad to read on the phone with the bank; she hid in a closet during an at-home meeting of Dad and the bankers. He told Miriam the house belonged to Weezie, and Bea used to scream, "It is mine! It is my house!"

I went into full battle mode, with Mike Simon at my side. He was preparing to go into court with testimony from Dale Bandel, Dr. Ness, Miriam, Nick and myself, along with a few others. The case seemed very solid. Then, a month or two before we were supposed to go into mediation and then depositions, Mike Simon called me to say that his firm Gunster Yoekley, also represented US Trust and the firm felt there was a conflict of interest and Mike could no longer represent me. Even though we had discussed this months before and they didn't think it would be a problem, US Trust felt there was now a conflict.

Mike told me he had arranged for a "killer" lawyer in Boca Raton to take over the case and that the new guy would do it on contingency because of the way the new trust was set up, Bea was barely giving me enough money to live on. As soon as the case got to the new lawyer, he reassigned it to his underling, Norman Fleisher. Norman was a nice enough man however he had no fire in his belly. Although I was told he would do a good job for me. It took a year for us to get into what should have been the opening round: mediation with Bea and her two sets of lawyers, US Trust and their legal team, and Gary Lickle, who was a lawyer himself, all on one side. It was to be all of them against Nick, Norman Fleisher, and me! No one suggested that Nick should have his own legal council since he was the remainder man on the trusts. I honestly didn't know he should and the other lawyers, bankers ALL trustees should have insisted on it if they were doing their duty as trustees, i.e. protecting the trusts and the beneficiaries but not one of them said a word. Not even the mediator who was also a lawyer. Afterwards I was asked "Why didn't Nick have his own lawyer?" All I could say was I had no idea he should, nor did he at the time. These people wanted to get rid of us as quickly as possible... that I am certain with hind sight! Was my hand picked lawyer in on that plan too? I have no idea but the deck was stacked against us before we even got started even though we had a massive amount of evidence that would have proved our case easily!

§

In the meantime, from January 2005 until January 2006, I spent most of my time fighting US Trust to give me enough money to live on. First, a few of my friends had helped me out before Dad died, since I thought I would be getting plenty of money when he went, but US Trust would not let me have money to pay off my debts. It took about four months of arguing to convince them to give me the money to repay the wonderful friends who had helped me.

Secondly, US Trust - directed by Bea, of course - told me that I would have an income of $1,000 a month. That was it. They would not give me a penny more. Dad had left me a six-figure sum. It was always supposed to come to me outright when he died but Bea had managed to put it in one of the two trusts that she, for the most part, controlled completely. There was no way on earth it would generate only $1,000 a month, but they were adamant: that was all I could have.

At the same time, my doctor, Professor Williams, told me that my Hep C viral load was high and he wanted me to go back on the interferon/ribavirin treatment. Certainly, the viral load increase was due to the incredible stress I was under. This was very expensive, running about $8,000 to $10,000 a month. US Trust refused to provide this. Nick wrote them e-mails that said, "If my mother dies, it will be your fault." After many tearful phone calls from me, e-mails from Nick and me and letters from Norman Fleisher, U.S Trust and the "trustees" finally gave me the money for my treatment, which I started in March 2005, but they still would not give me any more than $1,000 a month to live on. Slim pickings as I was unable to make any money on my own while in the midst of the treatment. It was as much a nightmare - although the players had somewhat changed, as I had been through before Dad died. Although Bea was obviously at the helm and she must have got some perverse pleasure in her continuing her torture of me.

This was my second time on the interferon, and it was not any easier. I had to give myself a shot in my stomach once a week. Once again the next day, I felt like a car had run me over. I was capable only of lying almost motionless on my bed. As the week went on, I felt better, but I was also taking mega doses of ribavirin, and this was making all my hair fall out. Much more so than the first time around, when I had been treated in Santa Fe. This time, I had a wig made from real hair.

Dad had left Nick a small amount of money outright, enough for him to pay his tuition at the American University in Regents Park and get himself a little apartment down the Kings Road in the area known as the Chelsea Beach. Alanna came over in the spring and went to summer school with him. It was wonderful having him so close that year, and we saw a lot of each other.

Ever since my divorce from Wayne, my son has been a star. He was my right hand at the island, helped me with my illness, went to bat for me with the bank, and was always there for me. I could not have asked for a better son. I don't know how I would have faced what I have without him. I don't think I could love him and his wonderful Alanna any more than I do. Meanwhile, the lawyers plodded along with the case against Bea, and mediation was set for January 14, 2006. I had been told that if the mediation didn't work out, there would be a deposition from Miriam scheduled the following day.

§

On Thanksgiving Day, 2005, Professor Williams told me that the treatment was working and that I had cleared the virus. I was over the moon. I still had three months more on the medication to make sure that the hepatitis was really gone, but my viral load tests were negative. It was a joyous occasion. Christmas that year was to be spent with my dearest friend Margaret, who had invited Nick and me to Walshaw, her Yorkshire estate, where we had spent a wonderful Christmas with her two years before. Alanna was spending Christmas in Virginia with her family, but I think because of my treatment Nick decided he should stay with me. This time around the interferon/ribavirin treatment was making me terribly worn out.

§

A few days before we were due to drive to Walshaw, I got my period, but it was not a normal period. I was haemorrhaging. My doctors found a polyp in my uterus. The bleeding was made worse by the interferon, which had made both my white and red blood counts fall through the floor. After much discussion with Professor Williams and my gynaecologist, it was decided that I needed to stop the treatment and take a heavy dose of hormones to stop the bleeding. This was not good news because I knew it would compromise the long nine month battle I had already fought and seemed to be winning. But I had to stop the bleeding and there was no other choice.

I went up to Walshaw with a box of adult diapers, the only thing I could wear to stanch the bleeding. I haemorrhaged for nine days. On the day we were to come back to London, Nick and I had a horrendous fight, and we continued to row most of the way back down to London in awful awful traffic. It was an insane day. Looking back on it now, I am sure I had been driven almost crazy by the hormones I was taking. Nick and I have enjoyed a good fight once in a while, but this one was epic - I have never felt so much rage. A heavy dose of hormones, 9 months of chemo and 9 days of blood loss had driven me over the edge. Poor Nick. He never flinched from supporting me.

The doctors decided that they needed my blood count numbers to come up before they could operate to remove the polyp, so they kept me on the hormones for all of January and scheduled the surgery for the end of the month at the London clinic. I probably should have cancelled the trip to Florida for the mediation, but I wanted to get on with it so badly. I was in no physical condition to go through the ritual. Adding a nine hour flight and 5 hour time change didn't help either. I was white as a sheet the morning we left for the mediator's office in Boca Raton, and I felt weak, not at all myself, but I was determined to go through with this, refusing to let Bea know my weakness. All the cards were stacked in Bea's favor. She had me right where she wanted me - hungry for my money to come out of trust. It was a lucky break for her, one of many it seems, to have me terribly ill at the same time.

That morning, Norman, Nicky, and I entered a large boardroom with a U-shaped table. Sitting across from us were Bea and her two sets of lawyers - first, Faxon Henderson the mastermind of her legal manoeuvring; Ed Downey, her attack dog; and then, US Trust and their lawyer (Gary Lickle joined in by speakerphone). Nick did not have a lawyer to represent him, and no one suggested that he could or should, even though he was only twenty-two years old and the remainder-man on the estate. US Trust and Gary Lickle as trustees should have insisted on this to protect him, but no one said a word.

Norman opened with a weak statement, not showing any of our cards - which made no sense to me. I had imagined he would say we had evidence, in Bea's own handwriting, of her manipulating my father to change his will. Dad's doctor, his long time banker, and the housekeeper and of course Nick and I. I thought we had an open-and-shut case against Bea, but none of this came up.

Instead, Ed Downey came after me, calling me irresponsible, uncaring, and untrustworthy. Once again, Bea had twisted reality to make it hers. I had thought it would be easy, but it didn't go the way I had pictured. The mediator was tasked, I am sure, to end discussion about the matter that day. Bea would let me have the money I was given at Dad's death out of trust, but only if I gave her both houses and all the money now in trust, from which she had been supposed to get income only.

At this point, we adjourned to a smaller room, leaving Bea and her lawyers and her back up team behind. I said from the start that what Bea wanted was not possible, that she was going to be found out as a criminal once the depositions started. She had treated my father no better than a junkyard dog, and she should be made to pay, but the mediator and Norman felt that it was going to cost too much money and that I should settle. I cried until I was blue. Nick told me to do whatever I thought was best. He just wanted me not to have to worry and to get the medical care I needed.

This emotionally painful procedure went on for fourteen hours. We were given lunch, then they turned the AC off, and Nick started sweating. By eight PM, no one had considered feeding us further, so Nick went out to get pizza. Norman Fleisher never presented them with Miriam's statement, nor did he give them copies of the scripts

Bea wrote. Those two things would have given us a huge advantage, but it was never taken. Even the witness list was not produced. Bea and her lawyers had no idea what cards we held and to this day have never seen them. It was incompetence and negligence or pure laziness on Norman's part.

Most of the day is a blur to me now. What I do remember is incredible pain. My heart, which I thought had been thoroughly battered and beaten, was now being stomped on, and in my weakened condition, I gave up. After all that time, I managed to get a little more money out of the main trust, while Bea got all the rest, but I got my money free and clear of her. At the time, it did seem to be a victory, but it was a hollow victory at best. Nick was the real star, showing that his love for me was foremost. Since all the money would have eventually come to him, he could have told both Bea and me to go to hell and to live within our means, but he didn't. He said, "Mom, all I want is for you to be okay, and I will be all right, too."

Bea and her team had been lying in wait for us. My illness made me so vulnerable that I had no fight in me. The lawyer that was supposed to represent me sat in the corner through most of the day and just kept saying "you should settle it's as good as you are going to do !" The document they made Nick and me sign is the most ironclad that any lawyers I've since showed it to have ever seen. I am unable to challenge it. The only way we might be able to revisit it is because Nick had no legal representation—which should have made it null and void, but somehow didn't. Nick could challenge it, but he would have to pay the court costs for everyone else involved, and it was all done knowing I was in bad shape, making it all the more dastardly.

In the beginning of this legal wrangle, Mike Simon, whom I thought the world of, had let me fall of the cliff when he stopped being my lawyer, My subsequent fall was broken by what turned out to be a very thin branch, which broke without my ever having a chance to hang on.

How woman was able to torture my dying father, manipulate his fortune even while he was alive and eliminate his only family from his life both in his life and after his death. The big questions about her had yet to come into my awareness. But what I know now about her criminal acts even before my father came on the scene continue to be uncovered. In the mean time it was time to get on with my life for a while trying to put all this behind me. It didn't stay there.

Chapter 7

<h1 style="text-align:center">Life Goes On:</h1>

The Sudan

Over the previous eight years, I had become best friends with Brigadier General James Ellery, whom I had met at a dinner party in London. Most of the time, he was posted to some far-flung place and we corresponded via e-mail. When we first met I was still in Santa Fe, and James was a colonel in charge of the British Army, London District. He had just returned from heading the UN mission in the Congo. For which he was awarded a CBE from the Queen for orchestrating the cease fire between the five feuding countries that had so demolished the Congo for so long. His next job was chief of staff for the UN in Sierra Leone. After retiring from the Life Guards, his first civilian posting was as the senior British advisor after Ambassador Greenstock to Ambassador Bremmer in Baghdad for the CPA (Coalition Provisional Authority).

James's typical "garden spot" jobs were not in places that I could or would even be able to visit, but his next job was in Juba, Southern Sudan, and a plan for me to visit was hatched that spring, after the mediation with Bea was over. In the wake of that debacle, this incredible opportunity came my way. It seemed as if the trauma of the past seven or eight years, since I found out I was ill and Dad started to go downhill, was behind me. This was a great opportunity. I began to keep a diary. Looking over what I wrote, it seems to me that the diary conveys the immediacy I'm looking for, and captures the day-to-day ups and downs of a very exciting trip, one that changed my life.

§

May 31, 2006
Into the Sudan

I am airborne on the flight to Nairobi. The BA stewardess has just handed me a bag of nuts that says "Out of Africa" on it. I have had to work rather hard to get into Africa, so this amuses me. Africa, the Dark Continent - with all that signifies. It certainly is all a mystery to me, and I am so thrilled to be heading there. I have so many ideas in my head about what to expect. The road to get here has been paved with obstacles, unusual occurrences, and laughs. I am expecting the same kind of surprises from the journey I am now on, but no snakes on the plane, please—I'm American!

The idea of visiting James in Juba came after listening to his many adventures over the years. My poor health never allowed me to even think of doing such a thing previously, but things had changed on that front in the best possible way. I had an all clear reading Thanksgiving Day, 2005. (I found out in the autumn of 2006, long after this trip, that the hep C had returned.) But for now as far as I knew the coast was clear !

When I suggested to James that I would like to see the Sudan, he agreed it was a marvelous idea, but when I indicated I meant it, he balked. After a bit of nagging from me, he said I could be of some help to the Juba war orphans, children who had lost their parents in the ethnic civil war that had raged in the Sudan since 1983. Once he put my trip in that context, it seemed I had a big green light. James was initially put off by my determination, repeating that this trip was not his idea, but I was not to be dissuaded. When the brigadier witnessed the perseverance and fortitude I had to reach the Sudan, he was not one to stand in my way.

James was able to persuade Alan Gyle, our vicar from St. Paul's Knightsbridge, to travel with me. The idea was that Alan would return later in the year to do his sabbatical in Juba or some other place in the Southern Sudan. Alan is smart and funny and has proved himself a first rate traveling companion. In order to avoid sitting in back of the plane in coach, he put his collar on to try for an upgrade out of steerage, but the Scandinavian woman at the BA desk was having none of it. He then removed the collar, so that, in his words, "I am not accosted by every nutter from here to Nairobi. The collar is a magnet for all of them!" Travels with the vicar are no doubt going to be fun.

I suppose I should go into a little bit about the Juba orphanage. When the UN arrived in Juba, some of the soldiers, led by Canadian Lt. Col. Mike Goodspeed (coincidentally from Kingston, Ontario, near my house in the Thousand Islands), found the property and its operations in poor working order. The building was dilapidated. It had no running water, no beds for the children to sleep on, and only rags to clothe them. Mike put together an initial charitable effort that raised $5,400 USD from his friends and family in Canada. He also arranged for the Bangladeshi engineers working for the UN in Juba to dig a well. Beds were ordered and adequate clothing found. He told me the children were so in awe of their new clothes that they put them away, so as not to ruin them, continuing to wear the old rags they already had.

So far, I have managed to send down another $5,500 USD from myself and a few dear friends who wanted to join the effort. From what I hear and have seen from photographs, the orphanage now has a new floor, a new coat of paint, bed (for all fifty-five of them, I think, with sheets), and the new well. There is much still to be done. Though a few are attending school already, it must be arranged for all the children to go. Tuition is $75 per year per child, plus books and uniforms. What we need to do now is make sure that the orphanage will have funding in perpetuity and determine the priorities.

The road to Juba so far has been paved with its fair share of misadventure. The Sudanese government decided at some level, whether it was in the embassy in London or from Khartoum , that Father Alan and I were not to visit their fair country, humanitarian aid workers or not. All kinds of hoops were set up for me to jump through, which I did with perfect grace, to no avail. The initial letter from UNMIS (United Nations Mission in Sudan) in Juba should have sufficed for us to get a visa, but when the consul for the Sudan in London saw the letter, he decided we needed another letter, one from the minister of interior in Khartoum. I had to defer to James, as neither Alan nor I had any influence or the slightest clue how to obtain such a thing. The UN in Juba was able to get the SRSG (Special Representative to the Secretary General) Jan Pronk in Khartoum to send a letter requesting immediate visas for us. James then tried through his friend, the US consul in Juba, Bob Whitehead, who got a letter from the US Embassy in Khartoum. That also had no effect. No explanation was given by Jena, my contact in the Sudanese Embassy in London. She kept saying the visas would come or they wouldn't. I planned accordingly.

Plan B was to fly by way of Nairobi and pick up a special "blue pass," good only for Southern Sudan, issued by the country's new governor. Bob Whitehead arranged this. The only problem with Plan B was that we couldn't travel by way of Entebbe, Uganda, which was James's choice for safety. He also favored it as a nice place for us to stay, on the banks of Lake Victoria, but Nairobi was the only place to pick up the blue pass.

That was settled, and tickets were purchased. Nairobi it was. The Hilton Nairobi was booked, and we looked good to go. Alan took over getting the visas from the Kenyan Embassy, with only one small hitch. I am not sure I can re-enter on the visa they gave me, as US citizens are only issued a visa good for one entry, but this can be dealt with in Juba, if need be. All this does make me wonder why America helps these countries. Wonder how much aid we send to Kenya every year? The Sudan is understandable, because unlike the rest of the world, GWB has decided to put strict sanctions on the government of the Sudan because of the massacre in Darfur. No other country has done this. Of course, the only country heavily criticized for Darfur is the US— for not intervening, but that's an old story that has become a broken record in US/world relations.

A few weeks ago, James mentioned the Mathaigu Country Club as the place he stayed for two weeks staging his heroic entrance into the Congo to break up the brawl involving the surrounding five nations over the Congolese wealth. Last week, my friend April Gow and I had dinner, and she suggested Alan and I stay there, and as great friends do, she and her husband, Roddy, booked us into the club as their guests. How fantastic. Something to look forward to when the snakes are crawling into my tent in Juba each night. James's description of this wonderful old colonial place promises four ball boys on its tennis court and two caddies for each player. Sounds like heaven. I may move in!

Yesterday, less than twenty hours and counting from departure, I got a phone call from the Sudanese embassy, saying, "Your letter has arrived, come and get your visas tomorrow." "Wonderful," I answer, "but we are flying to Nairobi tomorrow - it will be a bit too late" Quite a bit of pleading was needed to get Jena to allow me to come in immediately for the visa. I did not intend to tell her that we really didn't need them since we had found a way in the back door, so to speak, but I also felt that having the real thing would make life much easier for us as we travelled. I had to race to St. Paul's, pick up Alan's passport, and then go on to Cleveland Row and what should be a very elegant embassy directly across the street from Prince Charles and

Camilla in Clarence House. It's a nightmare, though, with old linoleum on every surface imaginable.

Once I arrived, I was made to wait forty minutes for some man Jena rang on the phone to get back to his desk. Finally, I was taken down stairs to the visa area. A mean woman named Mouna, who looked similar to the evil stepmother, told me to come back tomorrow for the visa. Back to square one !

" Please, can't you issue the visas now? Jena said you would."

"Jena has nothing to do with this. Who is she to tell you that?"

Of course, I have no idea who she is to tell me that. "She is the person I was told would help me."

The woman finally relented, saying that she would do it today but I should come back at four PM to pick the visas up.

"I am so sorry, but I can't do that. I have other appointments," I did not say—hair color taking precedence over just about anything else. "I must have the visa by 2:30 PM, or I will have to take the passports and leave."

Mouna was having none of this. "You are very lucky. We are doing you a great favor here. You have no idea how much trouble we have gone through for you."

She, Mouna, had gone to no trouble whatsoever so far, since she hadn't yet taken on the very difficult task of sticking the visa in our passports, stamping them, and scribbling something in Arabic on the side. She told me to sit down and she would call me when they were ready. I sat and waited patiently until 2:35 (past my deadline for leaving), and then approached her window. Very slowly, with a look of annoyance on her face, she rose from her desk and said, "May I help you?"

I was now aware of the reason for the glass between us, as I was overwhelmed with the urge to do some sort of physical harm to this beast of a woman. Instead, I put on my best, almost-in-tears voice and said, "I am going to have to leave. It's past 2:30 PM. I cannot wait any longer. Please give me the passports back, because there's no more time."

Mouna, with steel in her eye, glared at me and said, "We are doing a very big favor for you. You are very lucky. Sit down."

Just as I was about to bother her for the last time out, she came with a huge grin and strolled over to me with both passports in hand, visas shimmering silver. She wanted me to know exactly what a large favor she had done for me. Her accomplishment in attaching the visa proved this beyond a shadow of a doubt in her mind.

So what changed from a month of stonewalling to the abrupt about-face over the last few hours? A few days before, I received a call from a man in Harare, Zimbabwe, named Costas, who told me he was a "fixer". It seems that Alan had baptized the grandchild of a man who is the biggest tobacco dealer in Africa (James now tells me he is one of the biggest arms dealers). With ties to Mugabe, he was even named in Parliament as a bad guy. (Being named in Parliament means this man was absolutely up to no good.) Alan told him of our plight, at the baptism and the proud grandfather told him he would see what he could do to help since he had connections everywhere in Africa. After ascertaining the history of our travails, Costas told me he didn't think there was much he could do for us, since he was not well connected in the Sudan, but if I would like to be of some help with the orphanage, he might be able to do something for us. He was charming, and we had a fun conversation, but I told him that if the US Embassy and the SRSG couldn't get us visas, I had no idea what he could do. He agreed that I was probably right.

Then, yesterday morning, Costas rang and asked if I had heard from the Sudanese. I said I hadn't, and he said, "I think you may."

I thanked him, thinking there wasn't much time left so there was no real hope of a visa. A few hours later, Jena called. Costas had saved the day. Alan thought there must be some small child held hostage somewhere that forced the Sudanese to give us visas, which they obviously didn't want to do, but I think the answer was probably money. Amazing what baptizing the right baby will do for you. God must have been happy to get that little one in the fold.

Alan and the driver arrived this morning, ringing my bell and announcing, "Juba Express."

Big smiles were on all our faces, and we were on our way. I am now up in Club Class eating L'Artisan de Chocolat truffles (my favorites by the way) thanks to BA, my feet up. Clear as a bell over France and the Cote D'Azur, with a stiff wind blowing the entire Med is white. I have only spotted one boat out, rather large, but poor souls in those seas! I also had perfectly clear views of Sardinia and Malta, which looked like heaven to this sun-starved London dweller. According to the in-flight GPS, we are flying over a place called Ajbabyja in the Sahara Desert. Sounds wonderful. My first sighting of

Africa. What an amazing adventure this is going to be. I am a very lucky girl.

The desert below is just brown. Thousands of miles of brown. Fascinating. I'm fantasizing crossing on a camel—or perhaps a rally race across Africa would be more fun! The perfect trip for Nick and I someday?

§

We flew over Juba, but it was covered in clouds and I couldn't see a thing. After passing Darfur, which just looked like more of the Sahara—the landscape had changed, and there were rugged, jagged hills and greenish vegetation on the ground. I would see nothing else until landing in Nairobi. There are very few lights outside the city, and the airport is in a national park, so it was black all around. Since the population is very large, I assumed that the city is in darkness (t wasn't) because there aren't many electric lights. Arrival at the Nairobi airport, which was sort of 1970s modern, went without a hitch. Nothing notable in the airport, other than a sign I spotted for UNMIS flights. Of course they are not running for us at the height of the summer.

Our taxi driver, Joseph, was very jolly, and when we told him we were going to Juba he said, "Oh, it's very bad there. Still not agreeing."

I asked, "Bad how? Like we might get shot at?"

"Yes, probably," he agreed.

At this point, Alan and I could only laugh.

When we walked out of the airport into the cool night air, the

sidewalk was teeming with black people. Immediately, I felt that we were in Africa. The Hilton is dead in the center of town and the streets are full of people. There were big barriers in front of the hotel, manned with armed guards who motioned us in. The lobby is red velvet and marble - I am sure the height of chic decor for a Hilton in Africa. There are amazingly few white people, even in the hotel. I reconvene with Alan in the Jockey Bar for a drink, where we are the only whites.

I drink my ginger ale with ice and am slightly worried that I will be instantly ill from the ice. I then brush my teeth with tap water only to panic, a little too late, that it needed to be bottled water. I can see this is going to take some getting used to. I have brought cereal bars, dried fruits, and nuts, and I am bound to gain massive amounts of weight living off that stuff.

Not sure how we will spend our day tomorrow. I cannot connect to the internet from my hotel room so will go down to the business center and at least get my e-mails there. I feel even more cut off than I do at Walshaw. The room is at least clean.

When I got out of the lift there was an armed guard standing there. This is the norm on all floors. There is a big black hooker in a red negligee, standing in the door, speaking French to her departing customer in the next room. I don't hear anything else, being the civilized part of Africa, I can't wait to move on to the war zone.

Alan made the classic comment that he has never even slept in a tent in England. I feel the same way, but am up for anything. Glad the guard is out there; otherwise, I might wish I had a six-shooter. Now to bed for my first African night.

§

Friday 2 June 2006
Tent Nakuru, Juba, Southern Sudan

I am sitting on my private veranda in front of my tent, which is called Nakuru. Sounds rather glamorous ... it's not! It's six PM and the sun is starting to go down in the sky, the heat retreating. Sort of. Inside the tent, it is like an oven. I will open all the "windows" when we are out to dinner. Very basic tents. One small cot with mosquito netting over it. Sheets seem adequate, but if not, I have brought my own. Inside, there is an oscillating fan and one energy-saver light bulb. A camp chair and small table. Millicent, the manager, has brought me a hanging rack for my clothes; otherwise, I will live out of my suitcase. Outside there is a small covered veranda with a little metal table and another camp chair. Beside me is a large purple bucket that I thought must be for rubbish, but it seems to be full of water. What I am supposed to do with this water is beyond me. Each tent has one. (in hindsight I think it might have been shaving ? A personal sink of sorts ?) There is also a canvas bag on a stand that I now think is for rubbish, but not sure of that, either, as things would blow out of it if the wind were to kick up.

I am in the first row of tents closest to the mess hall. James requested this location for me, thinking it was safer. Alan is in the furthest row of tents, closest to the bathrooms. I would have opted for his location. My middle-of- the-night bathroom trek is going to be something. There are lights of sorts on metal sticks in a row, which I guess mark the paths between the tents at night. Millicent has assured me that there are no snakes about because they keep the grass and vegetation cut short. Never in my life have I known a snake to be deterred by short grass! My zip has a lock, which I will put on so the pythons can't self-open, as in James's camp (one of his many adventures), but there is a large hole where the bottom zip and the door zip open. I will stuff my rubber boot into it. That should work.

Also, since I'm right next to the mess hall, there is a bar and a large TV with the BBC blasting. No idea how long all that might go on, but it is Friday night. Luckily, I packed earplugs—I am guessing I am going to need them.

Yesterday in Nairobi seems like a million miles and ages ago. My view of the city from the window of my room at the Hilton left no doubt that I was in Africa. The hotel sits right in the middle of the city, and the buildings around it are quite shabby. The streets are teeming with people twenty-four hours a day walking in every direction through the traffic, on the roads and sidewalks. Helter skelter. From the ninth floor, they honestly could only be compared to ants. We were told emphatically to not leave the hotel unless in a taxi or Hilton vehicle. Do not walk around. Watching the hordes in the street over the thirty-six hours we were there, I never did see the head of a white person. My blond hair would certainly stand out.

We opted for lunch in the sun by the pool. I spent too long in the sun, being sun-starved after the miserable, cold, wet winter in London, and am now lobster red in the most uncomfortable places. I did some shopping at two stores in the Hilton and managed to spend plenty of money on gifts without ever leaving the building. Last night, I didn't get to sleep until about one AM, and the wake-up call came at 6:15 AM. Not a long night's sleep. I am feeling very tired from that, traveling, and the Juba heat.

I have not had internet access since yesterday morning, and it might be a few days before I can get into James' office to use his computer. Tomorrow we are off on a road trip with our own personal armed guard. (James has a meeting with the local governor.) It is supposed to be a very pretty trip.

Our flight to Juba was easy. Only thing to complain about was two rather pushy Danish men at check-in at the Nairobi airport. Much to my regret, they are four tents down from me, drinking beer with their huge shirtless bellies sticking out. One walked by me a few minutes ago and leered. Maybe more reason to use my lock than the possible snake visit tonight.

As I flew into Juba, the ground looked mostly flat, with mountain outcroppings here and there. Quite a bit more in the South, where we are heading tomorrow, so it should be an interesting trip in terms of scenery. The countryside is littered with round huts called tokuls (pronounced too-cools). Juba sits on the banks of the White Nile. James is very proud of a new bridge over the river that the UN Bangladeshi engineers built. It is the only bridge across the White Nile for a thousand miles.

Our plane landed, and we got that blast furnace feeling as we disembarked. One of James's military assistants was there to meet us, and he took our passports and got us through customs without us having to do a thing. I didn't have yet to show anyone my vaccination certificates. James told me I wouldn't need them on this end. Even the Kenyans did not care.

I was just visited by the most charming little girl age ten (?), smiling from ear to ear. A brown dress was falling off her because she hadn't bothered to or couldn't zip the back. She did a double take when she saw me and came up to me with a great big smile, without a word putting out her hand to shake mine and curtseying. Utterly charming. She was very shy but did try and tell me more than her name, which I think was Stella Tuku. She stood and smiled as I tried to make conversation. What are you doing? Where do you live? Do you speak English? All I got was the same big grin. She didn't seem to want to leave, so I kept trying. She eventually put her hand out and shook my hand again, and with the grin never leaving her face, she walked off. She was adorable. What a nice visit.

The natives, particularly the young ones, speak Arabic because the government in Khartoum imposed a law banning English in the schools back in the 1960s. The new government in the making in Juba has now mandated that lessons be taught in both Arabic and English. Perhaps a year from now my little friend Stella will be able to talk to me. The orphans too, I hope.

§

James met us at the airport once we were through customs. His driver, Edward, drove us in his smart new Land Cruiser to our camp.

It's newer than the camp where James lives, and according to him, the food is better. James had lunch with us in our camp, and the food was pretty grim. He went back to work and a very nice young man named Marcos, who is in charge of UN Human Rights Oversight in Southern Sudan, joined us. It was very hard to understand his thick accent, which was either Spanish or Italian, but he was charming and will be with us on our trip tomorrow.

We were then shuffled between two UN workers called Rune and Peter for a trip to the orphanage. It is much as I had pictured it, as I had received many photos in London. The children were darling, there was one very tiny one not yet two and a couple only two. Poor little things. Unfortunately, they speak only Arabic, so I wasn't able to talk to them, but I want to go back on Sunday and spend some time with them. James says he will walk me back after church. I will be happy for the walk, as we haven't moved a muscle since leaving London. Actually, not true—I swam two laps in the Hilton pool yesterday. Was that only yesterday?

Felicitia, who seems to be James's right hand, has a very impressive title that I can't remember, met us on the road for a trip to visit Bishop Mica, the large and impressive bishop of the Juba dioceses. He gave Alan a hard pitch for money. We were then taken to the almost-defunct Juba University with Arpan, a lovely young girl who is Bangladeshi, but was raised in Fairfield, Connecticut and went to NYU. We listened to the pitch from the guys at the university, which has been only a music and art for the past fifteen years . Because of the war, the rest of the university decamped to Khartoum, leaving this little place high and dry. The most remarkable thing about this visit was the oldest man, the President of the University, told me that his "first" family lived in the USA. His first wife is in Scottsdale, and his first son is Marine Vet from Desert Storm and lives in Baton Rouge. He was educated at Washington University and the University of Iowa and the other man was educated at Brown. All these details seemed bizarre, given where we were. We ended up spending more time talking about their travels in the US than we did the plight of this dilapidated old school.

Then Arpan took us on a tour. It's almost impossible to explain how poor Juba is. When James said these people have nothing, it was true. Nothing. The roads are so rutted and potholed that in places the Land Cruisers all but disappeared. James told me that at night the holes often become home to drunken Africans who pass out in them and then are run over because drivers can't see them. There would be no driving a regular car without destroying it here, although I did see a few. We drove by thousands of the round huts. Charming in the bush, but here in Juba, they are just part of the squalor. Many places were littered with waste and filth. It is not a place for the faint of heart, that's for sure.

The roads are littered with trash and crowded with thousands of goats, cows, and people. Africa is a country on the move, but here it seems it's only the women on the roads. They carry the most amazing loads on their heads. Giant buckets of water seem small compared to the load on one woman I saw, who had an enormous bundle of giant tree limbs on her head. Not just a couple—a huge pile of them. Must have weighed a couple hundred pounds at least. Talk about perfect posture.

We drove over James's new bridge. The river is turbulent and dirty. After seeing the squalor of Juba, I can tell you the White Nile is far from white or even slightly clear !

Going for a shower now before dinner at the US Consulate with the famous Bob Whitehead, of the Southern Sudan "blue pass" fame. Later: James arrived promptly at 7:30 to pick Alan and me up for supper. He let his driver go and was at the helm himself. The road to the American Consulate compound was the worst yet; at one point, we stopped abruptly, because if we had continued we would have dived head first into a five-foot-deep hole. The American Consulate compound was lovely. Quite unexpected. The houses were in good shape with lovely screened-in porches on the front. The place also sports a non-working swimming pool and a much-used somewhat run down tennis court, where Bob seems to host quite a few tennis matches. Dinner, cooked by a very nice American woman, was excellent. Their mess hall was a large screened-in building. We dined al fresco, under a half moon and stars.

We are in equatorial Africa - in fact, right on the equator. The Big Dipper is in the Northeast and upside down. On Grindstone Island, it is in the Northwest and right side up. This is about as far from Grindstone Island as one could get, but thankfully, growing up on the river prepared me to cope with the rudimentary life of my tented village, home for the next five nights.

§

Saturday June 3, 2006
Nakuru Tent, Juba, Southern Sudan

My tent's location, next to the open-air mess, where there is a TV and a bar that serves alcohol, is as I feared, definitely a problem. It's World Cup time, and the games play constantly. At 12:15 AM, after trying to sleep through drunken laughter and the noise of the TV, which is supposed to go off at eleven PM, I ventured out of my tent in my dressing gown to ask the viewers to turn it down. I found four drunk Africans, who I am sure are employees of the camp, not guests, as well as some white women. One woman immediately said, "It's too loud."

I agreed, and the rheumy-eyed bucks turned and glared at me. "Wasn't all this supposed to close down at eleven PM?" I asked.

One of them, smelling strongly of alcohol, replied, "What? This

is the bar, where we can watch the TV all night! You get out of here!"

I realized I probably should not have come at all, but I asked them to at least turn the thing down. They said they would, but they didn't. I slunk back to my tent. Blessedly, about ten minutes later, they turned it off. I think they thought better of getting in trouble. All but the one had seemed reasonable. I slept until about three AM, when the cleaning of the mess hall began. I took my first long walk to the bathroom at this point. I was pretty sleepy and walked right into the men's room. Luckily, it wasn't occupied. The bullfrogs were loud down there. Wonderful sound. I would love to trade Alan the frogs for the drunks.

Upon returning, I put in my ear plugs, which did the trick until about seven AM, when a couple of the cleaning girls came to remove their mops and buckets from the roof of my tent. No idea why my tent is the mop depository, but it is.

Up for breakfast with Alan, and at 8:30 AM, Bob Whitehead and an assistant named Jennifer arrive to take us to James's camp to get into our convoy of two Bangladeshi military protection units, one military observer car, a UN human rights group, and the Ellery/Whitehead vehicles.

Out of the squalor that is Juba, we started to climb to the base of the mountain nearest the town. Once there, James took us to the site of what will be the new UN center. It's high above town with a great view for miles around. Once out of the low-lying town, James is sure the UN workers will not suffer all the sickness they do now. It seems that everyone in James's camp, including James, which is next to the airport, has had cholera, and most seem to get malaria on a regular basis as well. Alan and I are taking Malerone to fend off malaria, which will not bother us for three weeks after the infectious bite, and hopefully not at all. I am using the hand sanitizer stuff constantly, because everyone wants to shake my hand, and cholera is everywhere.

After we see the new location, the convoy is off again. The roads at first are much like those in Juba, practically impassable. Better than the test ride track at the Land Cruiser dealer in Santa Fe! This really is the African bush.

Our journey today was to be exactly a hundred kilometers to Lanya. It took four hours to get there. We stopped a few times and once "visited the locals," where James had the SPLAM soldiers all laughing. I took some good photos of the gorgeous children.

On one of the stops nature called and not being able to just stand off to the side of the road and "go" I bounded off into the low brush terrified of coming on a snake. Luckily mission accomplished I came out and back to the road and immediately the head of the UN force was striding over to me " What where you doing?'

"I had to use the loo !"

"Don't do that again this entire area is full of land mines !! That was a very foolish thing to do. You are very lucky !!"

I guess I was ... but I had no idea.

Once we arrived in Lanya, James and Bob went to find the county commissioner, and Alan and I were sent to see the church. This, we can tell, is the way James gets us out of his hair. There is an endless supply of churches. This one was rather impressive, even with its roof full of bullet holes. John, one of James's two drivers, was our guide. We were joined by the local cleric, who told us that the bishop was away, but proceeded to show us his hut. And then sitting under a tree behind it, where five white women and one young man, Christian missionaries from South Africa. They were very impressed that we had five armed Bangladeshi guards keeping an eye on us. The older woman who seemed to be in charge then told Alan that my shorts were too revealing.

I said to the young man it must be nice to be in a country where everyone is already a Christian, and he replied, "But they are not born again, so we have our work cut out for us."

Afterward, Alan said to me, "I guess my baptisms don't count."

Unless, of course, one is in need of a Sudanese visa, in which case Alan's baptisms come in quite handy.

After an hour, we were all back at the cars and heading north again. Eight kilometers out of town, we stopped by the side of the road. Luckily, thanks to Bob Whitehead, we were fed a pretty darn good lunch. (James thought we had brought a lunch, but we hadn't. Luckily Bob was well prepared. Afterwards we shuffled who we rode with so that our conversations continued to be interesting.

What an amazing journey. The road itself has only recently been cleared of land mines. There are signs along the side of the road everywhere that mines are out there. Unexploded ordinance are also along the sides of the road. Many people carry machine guns and machetes. The place seems safe from the cocoon of James's Land Cruiser, but once outside the car you can feel a tension that might or might not erupt into violence at any time.

When we arrived back in Juba, James immediately waved off our armed escort, and we drove a bit until we came upon large herd of cows with giant horns. Texas longhorns have nothing on these guys. James and Alan got out and started taking photos. I sat in the car, mostly because I thought better of getting out in the middle of all those horns.

Almost immediately, one of the "herders" got in James's face and said, "You can't take photos of my cows without my permission." Even though the herders, who are Dinka, towered over him, James became his steely official self and replied, "Of course I can. This is a free country. I am James Ellery, head of everything UN in the Southern Sudan. You live in a free country, and I can take a photo of anything I want, and so can you!"

This seemed to be a sticking point, and John got out of the car to provide backup if James needed it. I wished the protection force were still with us. James was unfazed, arguing with the man until the situation was defused with laughter. Very well done.

Afterward, Alan noted how very differently he would have handled the man. He would have said, "I am so sorry. May I have your permission?" It was very impressive to see James in action, even if in this tiny bit.

We have been deposited back at camp. James will meet us for supper at eight PM. It's 7:25, and I need a shower.

§

Sunday June 4, 2006
Nakuru Tent, Juba, Southern Sudan

It's HOT. Only 9:30 AM, and I'm sweating. Of course, I am just back from a run with James to the American Consulate, where he was going to play tennis, but the court was already in use, so James went back to his office, or so he said, and I went off on my own and ran up the hill to Gerang's grave. General Gerang was the leader of the Southern Sudanese Liberation Army, whose now unemployed members we visited with yesterday on our road trip. Gerang led the Southern Sudan to victory finally in the dreadful war against the north an President Bashir. He was a great hero to the country. But very soon after the war was declared over he was killed in a plane crash. His grave is the Juba equivalent of the Washington War Memorial. A very important shrine.

I only slept about four hours last night. A very drunk African with loud radio placed himself at the table in the mess hall closest to my tent. About twelve feet from my head. This time I stayed in my tent but Millicent, the nice camp manager, tried to get him to leave, but unfortunately, she told the man that the friend of James Ellery, head of the UN, wanted him to leave. That brought on a tirade about the English and the UN being in his country. We were violating his civil rights, and he was protected under the Geneva Convention, he said. All I could think was please arrest him and then he can find out all about the Geneva Convention. Millicent was unable to make the guy leave. I lay there for an hour waiting, earplugs in, for him to give up. About 1 AM a fight broke out between this man and someone else. A beer bottle broke. I was pretty freaked. Then all of a sudden, I see a big black man—not the drunk—peering into my tent, saying, "Hello, hello, are you in there?"

I sort of shrieked, "Who are you? What do you want?"

He said his name was Kenneth. I kept asking what he wanted. He then said, "Do you know James Ellery?"

I replied, "James Ellery is my best friend. Do you want me to call him?"

"No, I am trying to get rid of the man with the radio," Kenneth said.

"Why don't you get a security guard to throw him out?" I asked. "They are guarding the gates," he answered.

"That isn't doing too much good if the problem is in here."

"You know James Ellery?" Kenneth asked again.

"Yes, he is my best friend. I am going to call him and get the Bangladeshi army over here if you don't deal with this right now. Do you want me to do that?"

"Oh, no, that won't be needed."

"I hope not," I said. "I can call him right now."

Amazingly, the drunk left, but I was so shaken by Kenneth peering into my tent in the middle of the night that it took a while for the adrenaline to dissipate. At about two AM, the cleaners showed up to clean the mess tent. All the bottles clatter into the bins, every chair gets moved. Finally got to sleep around 2:45 AM. The TV was turned on at 6:30 AM.

The funny part of my threatening to call James it that my mobile phone doesn't work at all in my tent. In a few spots it seems to get some sort of weak signal but not here. So calling him wasn't at all an option. But I wasn't going to let that cat out of the bag.

Obviously today I am fresh as a daisy today.

After making a stop with James at the consulate's tennis court, I ran up the hill by myself in the hot sun for about fifteen minutes with the usual local reaction. All the little children started waving and running along with me, big smiles on their faces. Some women were smiling, some were shaking their heads in distaste; all of the men looked disapproving. Passed four Dinka in full native dress. Their Sunday best, no doubt. They were very friendly. One old man who was walking said, "What is your problem?"

I don't have a problem! Maybe he thought I was running away from something or someone. I don't think the concept of running to fend off body fat has quite caught on here yet.

Most of the natives are Dinka or Nuer. The Dinka are very tall and thin. The Nuer men have scars across their foreheads from deep cuts they were given as boys; dirt was rubbed into the wounds to make the scars rise prominently. Some also sport slices, like sergeant's stripes, on their cheeks. One of the men at Juba University has mini-mountains in a line across his forehead. They look like giant zits, but since they are in straight line it's obvious they are not.

James will return at 10:45 to take Alan and me to church. Not sure what will come after that. Possibly an airplane ride. Definitely a boat trip up the Nile at five PM, then drinks on board as we float back down. Should be another memorable day. My tent is being swept and mopped under my feet while I type. At least the camp is very clean. Need another shower. Glad my hair is short. I don't have to do anything to it. It's wash and go. Even though the brown/orange water coming out of the tap is very suspect. Right out of the river I suspect.

The Juba Cathedral is being renovated. As best we can tell, the holes in the wall from shelling are being repaired and the building painted. It's a grand large building and quite cool inside. The preist who showed us around said they fill it with two hundred people on Sundays. Although church was held in another building on this particular Sunday, there were at least two hundred there. It was hot. I had James and Alan on either side of me, James in a suit and Alan in his collar and jacket. Sweat dripped off their faces. I didn't think it was much hotter than the Grindstone church and never broke a sweat. Must be all that running I am doing !

We sat with Felicitia, James's assistant. She is a bright, happy Kenyan who James thinks the world of. I can see why. We sat in a sea of Africans. The songs were jolly, and we all sang along. The service followed the Anglican Book of Common Prayer, and we almost had no need to read along. During the announcements, they asked visitors to get up and say a few words. Alan, of course, went up and introduced himself and me—thankfully, because James was prodding me to get up to get up there. No need as Alan was eloquent, as he always is.

The sermon was about making the right choices. Drinking or not, sitting around doing nothing or growing something—basic African issues, but I knew James approved, and because of that he managed to stick it out for the entire one-and-a-half hours. (He had threatened to leave after one hour.) After the service, we met a lovely Anglican woman priest, the African version of Grindstone's Aminta Marks.

After lunch with James at our camp, he went back to his office, and Alan and I had the afternoon to relax. I went on the internet on my little table in front of my tent. It wasn't the greatest connection, but it was working. Today, as I write this, the wireless is down. That's a good thing, as it makes me write in this diary instead.

§

At four PM, James arrived in his running clothes again to walk us to his offices to meet Andrew, who was going to take us out on the Nile in his fifteen foot outboard, which he brought down from Khartoum. The walk was interesting, going by large, old, colonial houses now all occupied by government ministers with many "guards" in front. We walked at James's usual fast pace. The temperature was well over a hundred degrees, and James said it could have been 110°. Thank goodness I had already gone running. Running early is helping me survive the heat. Alan, being from Scotland, turns bright pink and looks very uncomfortable, but he is enjoying this as much as I am, so there are few complaints from either of us.

We stopped by a place with a gaudy sign that said it was the Juba Hotel. It was once a finest shooting lodge in all of equatorial East Africa. It is now a hovel, but you can see the old tennis court, swimming pool, squash court, verandas and lovely shade trees in the central area. Ignore the squalor of Juba 2006, and you can imagine what it must have been like a hundred years ago. Actually, James said that until 1960, they wore black tie every night for dinner. Forty-five years of war later, it takes good imagination to visualize it.

We finally arrived at UNMIS headquarters, where we were put into James's car with his driver, Edward, who was directed to wait for Andrew with the AC running. Having slept hardly at all since arriving in Africa, I lay down on the back seat and went fast asleep. Was sorry to hear that Andrew had arrived, until of course, we got on our way.

We drove down to River Camp. Owned by the same company that owns and runs the place we are in, it is right on the banks of the Nile under heavy trees. Sounds lovely, but it was grim. Full of mine sweeping equipment and the tough Russians that do that job. Many SPLA or SLA soldiers. A horrible smell everywhere and I imagine the malaria risk is much higher with a swampy area all around. River Camp had been one of the choices for us to stay in. Thank goodness, we didn't; I couldn't have managed it. Dottie, the very pretty, blonde, blue-eyed woman who runs the camp, came out in the boat with us, and she told us every time it rains sections of the camp fill with six inches of sewage water. No wonder it smells.

The boat is a fifteen-foot deep Vee with a brand new 75 hp Merc on the back. It is "moored" to a tree under a high mud bank. It would have been right at home on the St. Lawrence. Dottie was a great addition to our group. Born in England, she is a nurse, and she has lived in Kenya since 1980. She has been at River Camp for six weeks. We pushed off from the muddy bank and ran upriver to the famous bridge. Andrew said that was as far south as we could go, because the army didn't like him going farther. He then turned off the motor, broke out beer, soda, and English cheddar cheese. We put up a little table between the bow cushion and the seat in front of the center console and had a most pleasant cocktail hour.

Once away from the banks and the camp, the sides of the river are sparsely populated with tokuls. Many African children swim in the Nile. Crocs are few in this part of the river, because like all the other wildlife, they have been wiped out by forty- five years of war. The river was full of eddies and about 1/4-mile wide. It got wider as we drifted downstream. The sun went down, the conversation was lively, and the air out on the water was cooler than what we had been in all day. It was a fantastic way to end the day, and I am sure will be remembered as a highlight of the trip.

Back at camp, James and Andrew joined us for dinner. James was in great form and told many of his usual eccentric and very funny stories. The mess hall was much subdued after the boisterous Friday and Saturday nights. Much less alcohol drunk. This was excellent news for me in my little tent next door to the TV and bar end of the mess. I went to sleep in a silent camp. Was woken by a minor thunderstorm at four AM, and went back to sleep until the bustle retrieving the mops from my roof started at 6:30 AM.

§

Monday June 5, 2006
Running with Tanks

Much cooler this morning after last night's rain. In fact, I had to turn off the fan and pull up my blanket once the rain came. I went right up to breakfast, enjoyed my usual porridge, and then went for a run. It was much cooler also because we are under a cloudy sky. I took off down the road that we walked with James yesterday. Much more activity, but very few cars. Children in uniforms walking to school. Many more "guards" out in front of ministers' houses. I decided I would be even friendlier than normal and said good morning to everyone. The reaction was better than yesterday when I was shy and not sure how to behave. I was even told, "I love you" by one of the young male guards. I use the term "guards" loosely, as I am not sure what else to call them. Many young men lounging around the front gates of the big houses.

The highlight of the run was two large, noisy tanks passing me. They rumbled down a residential street seemingly as fast as they could go. The many members of Southern Sudanese army was hanging off them. On the second tank, the man riding on its big gun was wearing a 50-Cent t-shirt. James would not approve. Nick, on the other hand, will think that's pretty cool.

It takes a lot of courage on my part to take off these last two days on my own like this. Mine is the only white face in sight. The general atmosphere in Souther Sudan is peaceful, but there is definitely an undercurrent that suggests all hell could break loose at the drop of a hat. When the two tanks came barrelling down the road toward me, I thought what the heck am I doing this for? But there are a lot of aid workers here now and the sight of a white woman running, no matter how many stares I get, cannot be that odd anymore.

Off to the showers. We are meeting with the dean of music at Juba University at ten AM and then spending the afternoon at the orphanage with a board meeting at three PM. James has told us we may dine tonight with the rather splendid Indian general force commander. He shows Bollywood films after dinner, which, James says, aggravates the Bangladeshis no end.

"He is splendid!" James says. Hope we are lucky enough to have the pleasure of his company.

Arpan picked us up at 9:45 to take us to Juba University. We were given another tour, which I videoed. The school is physically in terrible condition. Some work is now going on. The Mujahideen used it as a base camp up until just three years ago. Osama, where are you? After fifty years of war, strife and Sharia law, it's amazing that anyone smiles in this place, but very many do. There are also many sullen looks, born out of, no doubt, war-torn, abject poverty and disease-ridden weariness. It wears me out to watch them all scratching along with nothing. Our encampment with wifi (albeit slow as molasses) and flush toilets (a thousand yards from my tent) seems state-of-the-art, modern luxury in contrast.

The three old deans. One of them, more grey and wrinkly than the others took Alan and I into one of their offices and presented us with what they called their begging list. New buildings, a radio station— just the kind of things that Alan and I can pull out of our pockets at a moment's notice. They also said, "We don't want your money. We want you to build these things and give them to us when they are done!" I guess their grip on reality isn't all that it should be.

I answered, "That's going to be a little hard to do, with us in London." They took no notice. They told me that they would name the place the Louise Ann Ford School of Music. I declined, saying it should be the Father Alan School, since he is the music scholar, while I can barely hum a tune.

After the begging session (so glad it was their term not mine) we were taken to the main room for music instruction and were treated to two young men playing native instruments. They were wonderful—very African.

I loved it. And it was by far the best part of the show. The star violin pupil played a bad rendition of Twinkle, Twinkle Little Star, and a drummer whose drum had a huge hole in the front of it playing a rather jazzy song called "Juba." Thank goodness, I had the camera going, because the old deans made everyone get up and dance. Luckily, since I was filming I didn't have to.

Afterward, they took us back to the main office to hit us up once again. It came out at this point that they thought I was a Detroit Ford. Heavens help me; no wonder they thought I could build them a new school. I emphatically told them I was not one of those Fords, so sorry. I think they thought they had landed the goose with the golden egg and found out I could provide closer to a lump of coal. Not to mention the vicar is the one truly interested in their place, not me, but they gave me the full college try, nonetheless.

Back to camp and lunch. Shortly after we got to our table, a big man came up to us and said, "You are friends with the Big Man."

Yes, we replied, both Alan and me sort of giggling. He said, "Then you must help me and give him this letter." Alan took the letter, which was from some general in the SPLA, intending to give it to our friend Marcos, who is with Human Rights, because it said it was for UNMIS Human Rights. I suggest we actually should give it to James, since we said we would, and this man was sitting one table away from Marcos and hadn't given it to him on his own. James did take it, and I have no idea what he did with it, but it made the big man so happy that he came up to James and thanked him and also us for our help! Alan joined me in a good laugh at how puffed up our association with the

Big Man was making us when we really were of little value except for this lucky association with James.

§

After lunch, which consisted of some strange meat that was supposedly lamb—I am convinced it was goat since the place is loaded with goats - James took us to the UNMIS and briefed us on the mission, what they have accomplished so far, and what they still need to do. Amazingly, it's a very quiet place, for the moment - no doubt due to the firm hand of the General, as James is called here.

We then were introduced, through Rune Pedderson, my UN contact for the orphanage, to the astounding Augustina, who was dressed in the most beautiful native costume, all gold embroidery, and large puffy sleeves. Very impressive. We were then off to the orphanage.

This was a scheduled visit, unlike the other day, when we just dropped in. All fifty-five of the children (I use the term loosely, since there are four twenty-year-old boys) were assembled on the long front porch. They put the tiny ones, age two and up, in the front. Adorable. Of course, the kids had no idea what was going on, I don't think. We came with an interpreter because the children were only just now learning English. I felt like visiting royalty. They sang three songs to me, including, "Welcome Our Mama Anna."

They think that Louise is actually Louis and a boy's name, so they decided that I should be called Anna. Afterward, we decided they could call me Louisa. Needless to say, I was charmed and didn't expect it. They then made a rather formal presentation of four very good drawings. I asked if the boys who drew them could come up and sign their names to them. They were very pleased to do that. I had them explain what the drawings were of. I will keep them forever.

So much has been done, but there is so much more that needs to be done. They are incredibly proud of the beds, mattresses, sheets, and new showers they have thanks to my friends and me. They need medicine. Three of the girls were very sick during our visit—with malaria, I found out later. I told Augustina that she must go right out and buy antibiotics and that they needed to keep an entire medical supply on hand and replenish it every month. The pharmacy here, according to James, sells anything without a prescription. Morphine - whatever you need! Good thing, then, that we just need to provide the drugs. An old lady on site says she is a nurse so she can administer the drugs; they just need to have them on hand. I tried to stress that fruit and veggies should also be added to the beans and rice and the meat on Sundays.

We need to look into teaching the older boys a trade. The girls will marry, or be taken as household slaves. This is just the way it is, but the boys need to work to survive. There are about to be 400,000 soldiers without jobs now that the war is over, and that is going to make life here even tougher for these kids. I suggested, since trade schools do not exist in Juba, that we find people who can train the boys in carpentry, mechanics, and so forth to teach them on site. They will look into that.

The older boys were very excited to meet an American and asked me for a basketball hoop. How amazing, since it is exactly what I wanted these Dinka boys to have. (Nick, you need to come with me next time and coach them.) If we hatch an NBA star or two, that might just take care of the Juba Orphanage forever. The girls want a volleyball. A basketball hoop and a volleyball are available in the Juba market, and Augustina is dispatched to purchase them. They were all playing football (soccer) in a dirt patch across the street when we left, and these new sports will be something else to keep them out of trouble.

The other big issue is that there a quite a few pubescent girls, and the boys are probably full of testosterone. Augustina would like to see a separate girls' dorm built. I think the older boys should be encouraged to move on. The orphanage mandate is to house them until the age of seventeen, but I don't have the heart to throw them into the street, which is where they will end up, so for now they will stay. They need someone to employ them. I am sighing, thinking about trying to cope with all this from London or Grindstone Island.

§

Back at the ranch and about to have dinner with our UN point guys, Rune and Peter. James will, of course, join us. It's hot and muggy as usual, but there are thunderstorms around. Maybe tonight I will experience one of what James called "thunderstorms that feel like the world is coming to an end." Remember, I am in a tent—all the more exciting.

I have never lived so rough, and it's not bothering me at all. I had no idea I could manage this. One very good thing is that the place is spotless. Bathrooms and tent cleaned every day. Laundry taken at nine AM is back by five PM. Excellent. Maybe it's not that rough.

Dinner was with the Norwegians tonight. James, Alan, me, Rune, Bergid, and another Swiss. There were no meat and potatoes left for James to eat and no dessert for Alan, probably because this camp seems to have the best food; people come from elsewhere to eat here. Since we seem to be the last to eat every night, the pickings have been slim. I will probably gain weight being here, as I observed at the outset. Now that I am used to it, the food is not too bad.

§

Wednesday June 6, 2006
Last full day in Juba

I probably will not be rested, either, until I'm at the Mathaigu Country Club on Wednesday night, or until I'm back in my own bed on Friday.

The charming Arpan set up an early meeting with the Bangladeshi major who is the engineer in charge of work already done at the orphanage. That was very interesting, and I learned a lot about what still needs to be done, such as buying a generator and something to cook the beans and rice other than an open fire outdoors.

I spent the rest of the morning meeting with people from Norwegian Church Aid, whom Rune had organized. I was not in a good mood for this meeting, and Alan said I was short with the people. It was not their fault, but Rune, who had just been put in charge of the Juba Orphanage after two jolly Canadians, was not at all interested. He is a very serious man, and he has decided that the UN has done all they can for the kids; it's time they move on, he thinks, to another project. I told him that James had told me that the UN would oversee this at least until 2011. He doesn't care. He doesn't want to deal with the orphanage any longer, and tried to pass the money end of it off to this Norwegian church group, about whom I know nothing. I am not sending money here for who knows whom to administer. All I want to do is talk to James. As I am left full of despair after this encounter.

Luckily, James came to join us for lunch, and I was able to ask whether Rune's scenario was accurate. Absolutely not, he said, and if Rune were trying to pass the buck then he would replace him with someone else sparky enough to keep the energy going. I was greatly relieved. I hated to think that I had come all the way to Africa to be shuffled off on my own. I knew James was not going to put up with that.

Now I have to tell Rune to call off another meeting with the Norwegians this afternoon. I also have to get some money so I can have him go immediately to the pharmacy and buy medicine for the three kids who have malaria. That should have been done yesterday, but he didn't think it was that important. Aargh!

Rune didn't get my e-mail in time, so the meeting went on as scheduled. I told the Norwegian woman that I was very sorry to have wasted her time, but we would not need her, as the UN would stay on, no matter what. I told Rune that Jan Pronk, the wife of the UN head in Khartoum was officially the patron of the orphanage, and that the UN had to keep it because of that. The Mrs. Pronk part of the story, which is true, got me somewhat off the hook. His reply was that he would be gone in three months anyway, so it didn't really matter. Charming.

Nothing is easy in a place that has been destroyed by fifty years of war. There is nothing to work with. Without the UN to back up this project, I could never make it work from London. Luckily, James is on the same page. The whole experience with Rune has left me with a sour taste in my mouth.

The rest of the people here have been fantastic. They are the nicest people, full of energy and wonderfully dedicated. They seem to be an amazing breed. They give up everything they have to work in these hellholes, and they love their work.

Tonight, we dine with Bob Whitehead at the lovely American Consolate, where we ate on our first night. Coming and going form Juba, under the gracious auspices of the US State Department. Only one more night in the tent. Part of me will be sad to leave, but the other part of me, the part that is so tired from the lack of a really good night's sleep, will not be. I guess I could try to nap, but the World Cup is playing on the TV in the bar. All the employees are watching it. I refuse to complain again.

Alan has gone for a walk to photograph women with giant piles of sticks on their heads. We have seen lots of them, but we haven't been able to get a photo because we've always been in a car. He said if he isn't back by dinnertime, to send out the troops. My manicure and pedicure have taken quite a beating. Arpan says the Sudan is very hard on Pedicures, although she has a great one with flowers on her toes. I don't. Going to try to nap for a change.

Met Alan for drinks at 7:30 PM. He brought along a young Frenchman named Kim, who has just moved into the tent next to his. He lives in Kampala and works for a moving/removal company. He is setting up an office here to be ready for all the people they expect to populate this place. Everyone says that the change in the last six months is amazing. The changes in the last year, since the peace agreement (CPA), are remarkable. A year ago, there were no cars, and people were afraid to walk the streets. The Islamic government shot people almost for the sport of it, from what we have been able to gather. The Christian church had to operate "underground," and the priests at the Juba Cathedral said they all knew that if they said or did the wrong thing, they would be shot.

All that is over now. Everyone feels free to be on the streets. The roads in town are full of cars mostly belonging, of course, to UN or other aid workers—hundreds of white Toyota Land Cruisers and Nissans. The Japanese pay their dues to the UN by providing vehicles. The ones with the black UN on the side are, according to James, the "serious" vehicles, the ones belonging to the military. The ones with a blue UN on the side belong to UN workers, not military and therefore soft, or what the Brits call "wet." Many of the latter have signs on them: "No Firearms." In a country of 400,000 armed soldiers with nothing to do, I wouldn't think advertising that you are unarmed is the smartest idea.

The Sudanese for the most part seem happy. In a land where nothing really means nothing, they are full of smiles and handshakes at every meeting. Everywhere, we are offered bottled water and Coca-Cola - no matter how ramshackle the quarters. It is probably a good thing they are too poor to offer food. It would be very hard to turn down. The other day, I drank only a small portion of a Coke because just a little way through it, I started to feel sick. Not used to all those chemicals. I travel with my own water now, just in case Coke is all there is.

The bustle of the cleaning crews is all around me at ten AM. The camp is quiet, other than these diligent workers. The lawn maintenance guys wear orange jump suits. They look like American prisoners, though they clearly are not. Must have been a shipment of surplus uniforms from the US.

You see a lot of strange t-shirts and other clothing. Saw a t-shirt the other day for a bowling league in Cincinnati. You see lots of clothes donated to Africa by American schools and churches. I heard recently that because cheap clothing from Wal-mart and places like it in the US, the charities are overflowing with clothing. It should all be shipped here. Everything would be put to good use.

I find the task of helping care for the Juba Orphanage daunting. I am sure it is going to be full of challenges, not the least of which was the mini-disaster averted by my letting James know that Rune was doing everything he could to bail out of the project. James arrived for dinner and said, "I gave Rune a real blast this afternoon. Haven't done that for a while."

Oh, dear. I hope he finds someone else soon, because I can't imagine Rune is going to be eager to work with me now, but being military, he should take it on the chin and do a better job. I hope this is the case.

§

Dinner at the American Consulate with Bob Whitehead was wonderful fun. James was full of funny stories, as only James can be. In the middle of our meal outside under the stars (the stars not any better than Grindstone, I was disappointed to discover), a tiny little animal that he called a dik dik came up to the terrace. Bob went inside, got a piece of bread, and asked if I would like to feed it. It was adorable. Tiny spindly legs, about two feet tall, little twisted horns and a lovely little face. Perfect apartment-sized African animal. I wanted to take it home. I realized that this was probably my only safari experience for this trip. Other than the little goats and giant horned cows, which are everywhere, this is the only animal, I have seen. Animals seem to get exterminated in wars. I assume for food. Maybe if the human population comes back peacefully, so will some of the wildlife.

Our meal was finished off with peanut butter fudge squares. Giant Reese's cups—yum! James said he had never had peanut butter before. Not sure I believe him, but he enjoyed it with the chocolate! Food was better than I expected. I must have gotten used to the camp food, because now I find it rather appetizing. I am not sure however, eating the meat they serve. Even James says it's probably snake, zebra, or worse. Actually, I am convinced that no matter what they say, it is really goat. It all looks tough and unappetizing. Yet it's all James eats. He tried telling a humorless Swiss man the other night at dinner that fruit and vegetables were very bad for you, and he never touches them. I would have given anything to have a photo of that dour man's face.

§

Wednesday June 7, 2006 Juba to Nairobi.
From a Nakuru tent to Muthaiga Country Club

At 10:30, we were picked up from our camp by John, James's driver, and taken to the airport. John is a charming young man who studied at Catholic Seminary School, but decided not to become a priest. He has worked for James since he arrived on November 1, 2005. He told me he wants to go back and study at a university for his degree, but he doesn't want to leave Juba. I guess Juba University will have plenty of students if they can get themselves back on track. I hope Alan can be some help there.

We were left on our own at the airport and charged $90 to leave the Sudan. My passport is so full of Sudanese stamps it will be interesting to see if the US gives me a hard time going in and out from now on. I will find out soon enough when I travel back through NYC on June 23.

While cooling our heels in the airport waiting room filled with huge vinyl chairs that one could fall asleep in, I notice the place was full of giant Dinka, including one older man who walked with a cane who had to be well over 7 1/2 feet tall. Or more.

Rune came to say goodbye to us at the airport. He never let on that James had chewed him out yesterday and could not have been nicer. The tongue-lashing seems to have worked. I certainly didn't let on that I knew anything about it. It is almost as if he is a child who needs to be told how to behave. He will now, of course. The Big Man will see to it. I am sure he doesn't want to bring down James's wrath on him again.

James then dropped in just as we were about to get on the plane. I thought we might not have a chance to say goodbye. He carries a big black stick when he comes to the airport. Didn't see him carry it anywhere else. His general's baton.

The Juba airport smelled like a cesspool, and I was very happy to get out of there and get on the plane. Rather sad leaving James behind, but he is so happy and busy he will not even notice our having come and gone. The entire UN Security Council arrives in Juba tomorrow.

All fifty of them. And there are always the usual assorted skirmishes for him to worry about in the Northeast.

The Jetlink plane was very efficient and on time. Alan and I sat one behind the other so we both could have window seats. Wonderful views the entire way, but I actually slept for about twenty minutes, which just goes to show I am exhausted from all those mostly sleepless nights in the tent. Sleeping on a airplane in a little sit up seat is not my thing!

We arrived at the splendiferous Muthaiga Country Club by taxi. The building is old pink stucco with red barrel tile roofs. It's really beautiful. It reminds me of the Everglades Club in Palm Beach, with large open rooms all facing gardens. The grounds are huge, with a fantastic pool surrounded by enormous old trees. There is a bar and a little snack bar, and I hope to spend a good deal of my day there tomorrow. I have also booked a tennis lesson for ten AM. They actually have ball boys. (I have never played with ball boys before!) The courts are clay. It should be fun to play tennis and then flake out at the pool. Couldn't be further away from Juba. My room is lovely, overlooking large trees, with a small balcony. There are flowering trees and beautiful birds everywhere. The bed is large—what a change from the cot in the tent. There is a fabulous mosquito net around the big bed, and it all looks fantastic.

Alan and I have booked into the formal dining room. I will wear my pretty dress and he his linen suit. This is the anti-slumming-it part of the trip. Not nearly as interesting, but it does make Nairobi a lot more attractive than the Hilton, which was no great shakes, although I am glad to have stayed there and seen what downtown Nairobi is like.

Looking forward to our dinner. We have eaten well, but I think that white tablecloths and candlelight in the garden will be fantastic. Closest thing to it was the American Consulate in Juba. You always knew it was in Juba, and nice as it was for the Sudan, luxury doesn't exist in the Sudan. I very much miss a few of the people that we met. They were amazing. Arpan particularly stands out in my mind. I know I will go back. I was tentative with the kids, and now I wish I hadn't been. I should have spent some real time with them. Of course, the language barrier was a real problem. Looking forward to hearing a lot of "How are you, old chap," and the like in the dining room tonight. It's so quiet here. How nice not to have to wear earplugs to try to sleep. I can hardly wait to climb into that big bed.

§

Thursday June 8, 2006
Muthaiga Country Club, Room 13, Nairobi, Kenya

There is something about me, the number 13, and Africa. It really must be a lucky number. At the Hilton, on our way into Africa, I was in room 913. Now, on the way out of Africa, 13. If numbered instead of named, Nakuru tent would have been 13, too. No idea what it means, but I should make a point to play it in the lottery. Slept like a rock in my wonderful big bed. Only woke once by a text message from the local phone company, Safaritel, welcoming me to roaming in Kenya— at 2:30 AM. Phone switched off after that.

Dinner last night was lovely, and Alan and I ate for both Britain and America. Breakfast on the lovely veranda couldn't be prettier. Two tables full of young, white Kenyan/Rhodesian types with accents that are hard to place, laughing about the time they had last night— "Who went home with that lady, anyway?"—and then about who was going to fly or drive back home today. All quite bleary-eyed. I was happy to not be getting in a plane with one of them as my hung over pilot.

It all seems so exotic. This is the place that Karen Blixen used to send her staff to be trained. It is still the center of white African social life. The ambience is as genteel as any club I have ever been in, but no more so than many wonderful clubs at home. In many ways, this could be the Rochester Country Club, or perhaps a more tropical club, like Pink Sands or Cotton Bay, but there is the same feel, which instantly makes me feel at home.

Tennis lesson at ten AM—complete with the promised ball boys! Even the Palm Beach clubs don't afford that luxury. Then lunch, and spending the afternoon in the lush garden by the enormous swimming pool. I could not have gone anywhere further away, in every sense, from Juba. Almost feel guilty when thinking about how hard life is there. All those dedicated people working for the good of others who are so needy, with very little thought of their own well-being. No doubt, Juba has affected me profoundly, but the courts and my instructor beckon.

Tennis, swimming, sunning, and lunch by the pool, tea, and dressing for dinner: the order of the day at the Muthaiga Country Club. Out of Africa in style. Tomorrow night, we will be back in London.

Chapter 8

What Comes After:
London and the Island

After I returned to London, it was time to get ready for my summer on Grindstone Island. The night before I left, I went to a drinks party in Chelsea, where I met Peter McDermott. He asked me out, but I had to say, "Sorry, I am leaving for two or three months. Here is my card."

Peter and I started writing long e-mails to each other, and eventually we were on the phone together. By the end of July, he was on a plane, and I was meeting him at the Syracuse airport. This coming summer will be his sixth on McRea Point.

Life with Peter is fun, and we have traveled a great deal. He is the best thing that has ever happened to me. What a lovely gift my father sent me. Oh, that's right; he has the same birthday as my dear old dad, so in a way, I feel that my father must have sent him to me. He is also an engineer, like my father, self-made and working in the power generation business. He used to live in Admiral Rodney's house. The Rodney family are my very good friends from my early years in London, when I was in my twenties. Coincidences like this have made things between us an easy fit.

The second summer Peter was at the island, we were sitting outside on the deck with Nick, and we started telling Bea stories. Peter started asking about the estate. In the course of telling the story, I mentioned Bea's two different birthdays. Her real one, which she never celebrated while married to my father, and the one she put on her marriage certificate, with white out on date the original copy in the Palm Beach Court house and how she claimed this "fake" March birthday while Dad was alive. Peter asked, "How old was she when she married your father?"

"Almost forty-seven."

"And she says she was never married before?"

"That's what she always said."

Peter replied, "South American women who are even slightly attractive, and from what you say she was very beautiful, get married in their mid - to late teens. All of them do! She must have been married before your father, and this would explain the changed birthday."

It was like a bolt of lightning from the sky. It explained so much of Bea's weird behavior over the years. Including putting her hand bag in a drawer as soon as she came in the house and locking it. Now I assume so that no one would ever see her drivers license with her real May birthday. With Peter's encouragement, I looked on the internet and found Dad and Bea's marriage certificate in Palm Beach County. It had her date of birth as March 18, 1928. It looked a little funny in the internet then faxed copy and when asking about it to the woman on the phone at the County offices she said she could clearly see where Beatriz or someone had put white out on the date. She commented that she had never seen that before. I hired a private investigator who worked in Columbia. He was able to find her baptism certificate, had the May 18, 1928 birthday on it. This was the easy part.

On the internet, I found her nationalization papers to the USA from 1970 with the May 18, 1928 birthday. She gave her residence at this time as Park Avenue, NYC, although Dagmar Buxton, who knew her then, said she never lived on Park Ave, but out on Long Island the entire time she was in NY.

In Colombia, the investigator also turned up a brand new Cedula (the Colombian equivalent of a US Social Security number), it was dated February 2007 (after my father died and at the same time she put the house in Palm Beach on the market for $13M) for Beatriz Algarra Cuellar, signed Beatriz Algarra Ford. The address she used was fraudulent. She does not live in the house at the address given, and the people who live there said they did not know her, although she got some mail there. Chances are this is an address a lawyer used for her. Or friends of her in a past life. The house is in a very poor rundown neighborhood. Nothing like where the still aspiring Queen of Palm Beach would live. But maybe the neighborhood where she came from?

Also the number on this new Cedula is a number a young person currently 18 years old would be issued. Not a woman who at the time was 79! Where is her original cedula that would have been issued at the age of 18 in 1946? If she was married at by the time she turned 18 in 1946 her original Cedula would have been issued in her married name. Not knowing what that might have been the investigator was unable to turn up an original one. She didn't move to the USA until the end of the 1950's so she must have had an original number.

In Colombia, all weddings were church weddings until the mid-1970s. There was no such thing as a civil wedding. Each marriage was registered at the individual church; amazingly, there is no central database. Also, until the mid-1970s, there was no such thing as a divorce in Colombia, so there is no way that in early 1974, Bea could have had gotten a divorce, but going from church to church is an almost impossible task, particularly if I have to pay a private investigator to do it.

The more I run this by professionals and friends, there is no other explanation for her changing her birthday on her marriage certificate to my father, no other reason for hiding her handbag and locking it in a drawer as soon as she came in the door for thirty years. No other reason for making a big deal about of being a Pisces ... and also why their wedding so was so on the Q-T.

Marriage records in NY State are sealed as long as one party is alive, so we can't search to see if there might have been a wedding earlier than her "debut" in 1957 at the International Debutante Ball— at twenty-nine years old. A little past the sell-by date for a deb. A friend in NYC searched NY Times records for announced weddings in NY and found no mention of her.

One of the investigators looked through a few Colombian newspaper archives from the mid-1940s to mid-1950s, but found nothing. Of course, we have no idea where she actually lived or what newspaper would have carried it—if it even appeared in a newspaper.

When my editor called Bea to ask why she has two different birthdays on legal documents, she got very upset. She said that it was private and she didn't speak about private things on the phone and promptly hung up. Bea continues to pursue her social Palm Beach and Newport existence. Unable to sell the Palm Beach house due to the recession, she is still living in it. The price is reduced now to $4,995,000—and still not moving.

Peter thinks she will have a Scrooge moment and realize that if she wants to go to heaven, she needs to make things right with me. I am not holding out much hope for someone who is so truly evil to recant and make it right. I live with some hope, but I also buy lottery tickets. One or the other might hit.

After receiving the email from Bea's lawyer using the wording that Mrs. Ford and her family do not agree to the publication of the "<u>facts</u>" in Louise's book I put it, in the prologue, I was encouraged to contact a new investigator in Colombia so as we go to print the search for the truth continues.... Bea has been given copies of the book before printing and I know she has seen the printed version. She is never attempted to deny bigamy. If anyone doubts the story I have told in the book all one needs to look at is Miriam the housekeepers affidavit, and Bea's hand written notes that follow in the Appendix at the end... But for now the mystery remains and the more I find out, the more questions there are!

The End

For now...

Appendix
Miriam's Affidavit

STATE OF FLORIDA 1) ss: COUNTY OF PALM BEACH)

I, Miriam Sabillon, being duly sworn, depose and say as follows:

1. I am over the age of 21 years, and am competent to make this affidavit. I make this affidavit based upon my personal knowledge of the facts contained herein.

2. I have been promised no compensation for providing this affidavit and have no financial interest in the outcome of any litigation between Louise Ford and the Estate and Trust of George Ford.

3. Prior to George Ford's death, I was the housekeeper for George and Bea Ford. I began working for the Ford's approximately 8 years ago. I generally worked every day Monday through Saturday. Sunday was my day off.

4. Over the last year of George Ford's life, my role in the Ford home was greatly expanded. Bea requested that I spend the night in their home and apartment to take care of George. At Bea's request, I bathed George, gave him his medications, helped him use the bathroom, and generally assisted him with daily living. My increased role began in May of 2004. In September of 2004, I began staying with George and Bea every night.

5. I essentially lived with the Fords from September 2004 through the date of George Ford's death December 24, 2004. The only time I left the residence was between 3 p.m. and 9 p.m. when an aide came to the house. I worked seven days a week.

6.   I have no medical training or experience in the health care industry.

7.   During my time working for the Fords, George's mental capacity deteriorated greatly.

8.   For at least the last three years of George's life, he appeared to me to lack capacity. I observed many incidents in which George was confused and disoriented.

9.   For example, I specifically recall a telephone call from Bea. I was home alone with George and he picked up the phone. He told Bea that he was at the store shopping when he was clearly at home. He began asking me who I was. The phone call may have been 5 years ago.

10.   For at least the last three years, George would sit around and spit on the floor of his home. This infuriated Bea. One time she stepped in his spit and used alcohol to get the spit off her foot. He spit on the floor routinely. It was not isolated to single incidents.

11.   During my time at the home, George lost interest in reading the newspaper. Bea would have me give him the paper most mornings. However, he would simply glance at it and put it aside.

12.   I recall on several occasions, George would look outside and tell me how the weather was in New York. He appeared to me to be completely making it up.

13.   One time, Bea went to visit her sister in Sarasota. Bea called the house and George answered the phone. He told her he was at a rifle store. I got on the phone with Bea and she told me what George had said. This was over two years ago.

14.   Sometimes Bea would go out and leave me with George. George would tell her he was all alone when I was with him the whole

day. Bea would accuse me of leaving the home, which was not true. George did not know what he was talking about.

15. George could not remember things. He would often forget that he ate breakfast. He would forget whom he spoke with on the telephone and whom he met with.

16. The serious downturn in his mental capacity began after 2000. He began to not take care of himself. His hygiene became poor.

17. During the last months of his life, he became even worse. He started to tell me about a son named Edward, which I know he did not have.

18. George always spoke fondly of Weezie and Nick. He called Weezie a good, good daughter. He told me "this house is Weezie's house." He talked about Weezie and Nick constantly. He said that Weezie looked like him. He seemed proud of her.

19. George always got excited when the phone rang, because he thought it was Weezie.

20. Bea would often not let Weezie talk to George. Bea instructed me to never pass the phone to Mr. Ford. I was not allowed to let George speak with Weezie.

21. Bea often told Weezie that George was sleeping when he was right there.

22. On November 9, 2004, I gave the phone to Mr. Ford. Weezie was on the line. Bea found out, was mad, and accused me of hiding things.

23. George got excited and happy when he spoke to Weezie.

24. Bea tried to tell me that George should not talk to Weezie because it upset him. This did not appear to be the case. Just the opposite was true.

25. On many occasions, I had to act as if I was picking up the phone and talking on the phone in George's presence because I knew that Weezie was on the line and I was not allowed to let her talk to George.

26. Every once in a while, Bea would allow Weezie to speak, but she usually made excuses.

27. Bea told me that she lied to Weezie about George being asleep.

28. Bea accused Weezie of calling for money. She told George that Weezie was only after his money and that was the only reason she called. George would get mad at Bea when she said that.

29. Bea also told George that Weezie was lying about being sick. Bea said that she had a brother who was doctor, and the brother said that Weezie was lying.

30. I observed on many, many occasions Bea prepping George for meetings with his bankers and lawyer.

31. She yelled at George after he spoke to someone important. She got mad at him when he forgot what he was supposed to say to the lawyers and bankers.

32. During the last few years of George's life, he had trouble dialing the telephone. I do not think he could dial the phone at all during the last couple of years of his life.

33. Around Christmas 2003, the floors had recently been painted in the home. George spit on the floor as he usually did. Bea said, "I'm spending a lot of money fixing these floors." George said, " This money is mine and Weezie's." He told her that this house was Weezie's house.

34. Bea was very afraid that George was going to change his estate planning documents.

35. When the house was being painted, George asked me if I had a car so that I could take him to the bank to change his will. He wanted to cut Bea out of the will and give his money to Weezie.

36. Bea told me to tell him that my car was broken when he wanted to go to the bank. She told me never to take him to the bank. He would get upset with me about it.

37. Bea also made excuses for not taking him to the bank, such as the bank is closed, it is a holiday, etc. when it was not true.

38. Recently, George complained that he had no money. Bea went to the bank and changed in money for a bunch of one- dollar bills to fill his wallet she he would think he had money.

39. On December 16 2004, Bea's brother came to the house and took George's checkbook with Bea. I am not sure if they took any money.

40. Bea told me in April of last year that she was going to have Nick removed from George's trust. Bea prepared papers for George to use to prepare for his discussion with the lawyers and bankers. A true and correct copy of the papers are attached. Bea's handwriting appears on the papers.

41. Bea said that she did not want to have anything to do with Nick. She said she wanted the grandson out of the trust.

42. Bea told me that the document George signed would be invalid if Bea was present when it was signed.

43. Bea told me to stay for the meeting with the bankers and help George.

44. Before the bankers came to sign the new document, Bea pretended she was leaving. She yelled, "Bye, sweetie" to George. She then hid in the closet while the meeting took place so that she could hear what was being said. She told me that she was going to be hiding in the closet.

45. The meeting took place in the second, smaller dining room. Bea hid in the closet in the larger dining room, where the china is kept. The door to the closet was hidden by a screen. I went to get Bea after the bankers left.

46. Bea was mad when she finally got out of the closet because she could not hear what happened during the meeting. She said that she should have put a tape recorder nearby.

47. Bea told George what to say before the meeting. George was confused and out of it when he signed the documents that day. I was present when the documents were signed.

48. Bea told me that if the bank knew that she was prepping him, the document would be invalid.

49. That was not the first time I observed Bea prepped George. Bea prepped George for many, many meetings with his bankers and lawyers. She always told him what to say before everyone got there. However, George's words usually did not come out the way Bea prepared him, because he forgot. This made Bea mad. Sometimes she would cry.

50. One time, after Weezie left, Bea prepared George to speak with his lawyer. I do not remember what he was being prepped for.

51. Bea called the bank herself to tell them that George wanted his grandson out of the documents.

52. Bea told me that she got herself put on George's checkbook toward the end of his life. She told me that she had George sign a number of blank checks in case anything happened to him.

53. Bea told George to stop giving Weezie and Nick money. She told George that they did not have the money to help Weezie and Nick, and that they would be penniless. George wanted to send Weezie money. Bea said they could not afford to. Bea prepped

George to say to Weezie that he had many, many years to live and that he needed the money for his own medicines.

54. Bea began saying these things to George before Weezie moved to London.

55. Sometimes Weezie would fax a list of her expenses. Bea would not let George pay them or would only let him pay a portion. She was constantly telling George that Weezie was not sick.

56. Bea also told George not to pay for Nick's tuition. She said that Nick was a brat.

57. I was present at the house one time when George and a bank officer were discussing the Newport residence. The bank officer came to George's home. They asked how the property would be owned. George said my name and Weezie's name. Bea was walking into the room when she heard him say that. She was furious. She yelled, "Over my dead body, over my dead body." She threatened George with divorce. Dale was not there. It was another bank representative.

58. Over the next few days, Bea yelled at George and threatened to divorce him if he put the property in Weezie's name. I was in the kitchen while they were arguing. George wanted to put the property in Weezie's name.

59. Bea often threatened divorce to get what she wanted. She would leave the house after some of the arguments, and George would be afraid she was not coming back.

60. Bea also flirted with George to get what she wanted. One time, she was wearing a tennis dress. She told me she was going to flirt with George and get him to sign something. I cannot remember what it was.

61. During the last year of George's life, Bea refused to spend money on things for George. I told Bea that George needed a new pair of slippers so he wouldn't fall on the floor. Bea refused

to buy them and said his old ones were fine. Bea would go to the store on Sundays and buy food. She told me that the food for George had to last the whole week. It was not enough for George, but she told me it had to last. I have attached a note from Bea talking about the groceries.

62. Bea and I talked about giving George fish, which was supposed to help his memory. However, Bea would only let me give it to him once or twice a week because it cost too much.

63. Bea was mad at Dr. Ness after he wrote the letter concerning George's capacity. She changed doctors after the note was sent.

64. Bea locked George out of her bathroom and the guest bathroom because she did not want him to use them.

65. Bea stopped sleeping in the same room with George more than a year before his death. One night, while they were living in the apartment after the hurricane, George got lost and sat on Bea's bed. Bea screamed at him to get out. She said she would take him to the hospital.

66. She threatened to take him to the hospital sometimes to get what she wanted. Mostly, to get him to stay out of her bathroom and stop spitting on the floor.

Bea's Hand-Written Notes

Bea's hand written notes for George to read to his lawyer to change his trust documents.

4TH AMENDMENT

2nd paragraph

change Nicholas

George Grant

— grandson —

X

BRAD GREER

659 — 4040

REVOCABLE TRUST

FOUR AMENDMENT OF
MAY 20, 2003
ELIMINATE NICHOLAS
GEORGE GRAND

PUT IN HIS PLACE
BRAD GREER

JIMMY PRESSLY
659-4040

TRUST

FOUR AMMENDMENT

~~CHANGE~~

ELIMINATE

NICHOLAS GEORGE GRANT

AND IN HIS PLACE

PUT BRAD GREER

659-4040

This is a letter Bea wrote to an attorney named Levy asking him to change the names on the deed to 300 Regent Park for Dad to sign. He was almost ninety-four years old when this letter was written. I found it in the box of legal papers recently. I had never seen this before but the lawyers had it. There so much evidence that I was never aware of ... so much that was never used.

```
Palm Beach February 4, 2000

Mr. Bryan Levy
GLANTZ & GLANTZ
7951 S.W. 6th Street Suite 100
Plantation, Florida 33324

Dear Mr. Levy:

As per instructions from your colleague, the
Attorney Ivan Saborio, I am enclosing copy
of the Deed to our house in Palm Beach.

The deed was signed by my husband when we
bought the property but I was not included.
Now my husband has agreed to include me in
his deed.

I am enclosing check in the amount of $150.00
to cover the cost of making the deed.

Would you please send me back the original
together with the new one so we would have
it certified and registered.

Please send them to me by Federal Express.  Our
account number is  1293-4009-6 "Thundercroft"
at our address 300 Regent Park, Palm Beach,
Florida 33480.

Many thanks.
```

Mrs. George E. Ford

Mrs. George E. Ford
Member of Prepaid Legal Services

This is the way Dad had always wanted it. Chase (was Dale Bandel). Dad's was fair.   His lawyers knew this yet they let such radical changes take effect even while he was alive not caring what he wanted. No one protected him, his wishes, mine or my son's. The only winners in the end were "his wife" and the lawyers.

MEMORANDUM

TO:	Trent S. Kiziah
FROM:	James G. Pressly
RE:	George Ford
DATE:	April 24, 1992

Trent,

Mr. Ford is pleased with the Will and Trust. The only chanage that he wants to make in the trust is that the successor-trustee should be Chase and his wife and his daughter. He is planning to sign on Monday.

Thank you.

JGPjr/mj

Made in the USA
Charleston, SC
23 February 2012